THE BEST OF MELISSA JO REAL RECIPES

MAKE IT

MELISSA KAUPER

Introduction

Welcome to the kitchen of Melissa Jo Real Recipes! I created this book for YOU because without my followers and fans my dream of sharing my most beloved family recipes would not be possible. I have curated a book full of family recipes, fan favorites, and viral sensations from the past four years of me sharing recipes on social media. I purposefully put together your favorites which include my best Italian recipes from my grandmother, my mother, and me, quick and easy downright delicious one pot meals, 30 minute meals for my friends who are just like me busy busy, and of course some crowd pleasing party favorites. It is with extreme pleasure and delight that I present the BEST of Melissa Jo Real Recipes so you can Make It!!!

Contents

INTRODUCTION	3
ITALIAN FAMILY FAVORITES	**6**
STUFFED ARTICHOKES SICILIAN STYLE	8
BAKED ZITI	10
SUNDAY SAUCE	12
GRANDMAS JO'S MEATBALLS	14
LASAGNA	16
RAGU SAUCE	18
LASAGNA SOUP	20
RIGATONI ALLA VODKA	22
CHRISTMAS EVE SHRIMP LINGUINE	24
SHRIMP SCAMPI	26
LINGUINE & CLAMS	28
PASTA FAGIOLI	30
BACON CARBONARA	32
GRANDMAS ARTICHOKE QUICHE	34
ONE POT MEALS & SOUPS	**36**
CHICKEN POT PIE SOUP	38
MARRY ME CHICKEN SOUP	40
ONE POT CHICKEN PAPRIKA	42
ONE POT CHICKEN & DIRTY RICE	44
MISSISSIPPI CROCK POT ROAST	46
CHILI	48
EASY CHEESY ROTINI BAKE	50
ONE POT BEEF STROGANOFF	52
ONE POT UNSTUFFED PEPPERS	54

CREAMY SAUSAGE TORTELLINI SOUP	56
30 MINUTE MEALS	**58**
ROASTED TOMATO RICOTTA PASTA	60
EASY BOURSIN CHICKEN BAKE	62
COPYCAT OUTBACK ALICE SPRINGS CHICKEN	64
GREEK CHICKEN & TORTELLINI	66
ONE POT CHICKEN & LEMON RICE	68
JIFFY JOES	70
CHICKEN PICCATA	72
EASY BEEFARONI	74
CRAB STUFFED SALMON	76
ONE POT CREAMY STEAK PASTA	78
PARTY PLEASERS	**80**
CROCKPOT SPINACH ARTICHOKE DIP	82
EASY ONION DIP	84
ROAST BEEF & AJU SLIDERS	86
BIG MAC SLIDERS	88
SAUSAGE & PEPPERS SLIDERS	90
PIZZA SLIDERS	92
EASY CHEESY GARLIC BOMBS	94
EASY ARTICHOKE DIP	96
BIRDIE SANDWICHES	98
DESSERTS	**100**
CANNOLI POKE CAKE	102
APPLE PIE	104
TIRAMISU POKE CAKE	106
HOT COCOA POKE CAKE	108
KEY LIME PIE	110
PINEAPPLE UPSIDE DOWN BUNDT CAKE	112
ACKNOWLEDGEMENTS	**114**

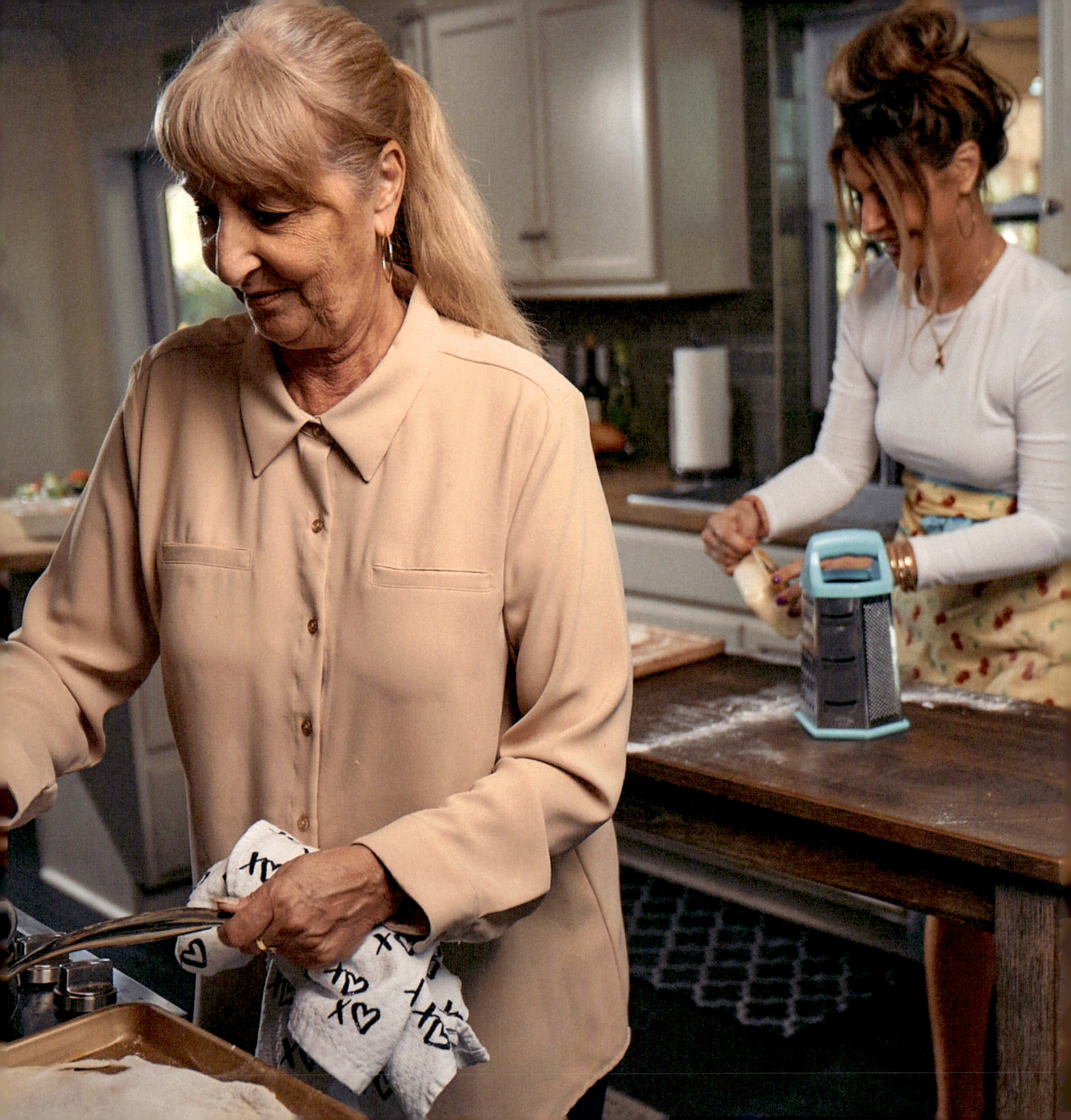

Italian Family Favorites

STUFFED ARTICHOKES SICILIAN STYLE

SERVES 6

INGREDIENTS

6 artichokes

2 lemons

water

1.5 cups Italian style breadcrumbs

½ cup of grated Locatelli Pecorino Romano Cheese

About 1 bulb of garlic (each clove peeled and cut lengthwise into slivers)

½ cup of chopped fresh Italian flat leaf parsley

about ½ cup of extra virgin olive oil

Kosher salt and cracked black pepper plenty of it!

1 stick of butter melted and rationed out into servings for each person to use for dipping. about 1-2 tbsp. of melted butter per person

DIRECTIONS

1. First, follow the steps below on "How to Prepare and Clean Artichokes".

2. Peel a bulb of garlic and separate into cloves. Cut each clove into about 3-5 slivers lengthwise depending on the size of each clove. You will use about 1/4 of the slivers of garlic in the breadcrumb stuffing and 3/4 of the slivers of garlic directly into the leaves of the artichokes.

3. Breadcrumb stuffing: In a bowl add the Italian breadcrumbs, grated Pecorino Romano cheese, fresh chopped parsley, plenty of kosher salt and cracked black pepper (at least 1 tsp. of each), about 10-15 slivers of garlic, (Save the rest of the garlic slivers for stuffing the artichokes) & about 2-3 tbsp. of olive oil just to moisten the breadcrumbs. Mix all together with a spoon.

4. After the artichokes are dry, spread open the leaves and begin adding 1 sliver of garlic into about every other artichoke leaf. Then, take spoonfuls of the breadcrumb mixture and sprinkle into the artichoke leaves. Spread open the artichoke leaves so the breadcrumb mixture gets down into the leaves. Sprinkle over the top of the artichoke as well. Repeat for each artichoke.

5. In a large stock pot or Dutch Oven, fill the pot with water about halfway up the pot.. Add the lemon peels into the pot of water. (the lemons you previously squeezed into the water to clean the artichokes) Add the stuffed artichokes into the pot of water. The water line should come up to about the halfway mark of each artichoke.

6. Drizzle each stuffed artichoke with plenty of olive oil. About 1-2 tbsp. of oil drizzled on each. Then, season the top of each artichoke liberally with kosher salt and pepper.

7. Bring the pot of water to a rolling boil. Once the pot of water is boiling lower to a low simmer and cover the pot completely. Steam the artichokes for about 40-45 minutes or until the leaves of the artichokes easily come loose from the base when you tug on them.

8. Remove the artichokes and place into a serving dish family style or serve each in an individual separate bowl. Melt the butter and give each person about 1-2 tbsp. of melted butter in a ramekin.

9. You eat the artichokes by plucking each leaf, dipping in the melted butter and scraping the fleshy artichoke and stuffing off of each leaf with your mouth.

10. Once all the leaves are gone. you will get to the bottom of the artichoke which is the heart. Pull away the little stems (like green little hairs) and reveal the heart. Dip the heart into the melted butter and savor the BEST PART! However, this can be highly debated. LOL

11. ENJOY!

HOW TO PREPARE AND CLEAN ARTICHOKES:

1. First, cut off the bottoms to make the artichokes stand upright on their own without wobbling.

2. Then, cut the tops off the artichokes, so you can spread open the leaves to stuff.

3. Next, using kitchen shears snip off any of the pointy, sharp, hard tops of the leaves.

4. Fill a bowl with water and squeeze two lemons into the water. (Save the lemons after you squeeze them for the cooking process.) Then, add the artichokes top side down into the lemon water and let them soak in the water for about 5-10 minutes. Finally, remove them from the water, spray them with fresh water, and place them top side down onto paper towels to drain, drip, and dry before stuffing and cooking!

BAKED ZITI

SERVES 6-7

INGREDIENTS

1 lb. ziti pasta

1.25 qts homemade sauce or Rao's tomato basil sauce

32 oz. Ricotta

14 oz Polly-O mozzarella cut into little one inch cubes

Cracked black pepper and salt

¾ cup Locatelli Pecorino Romano grated

Fresh chopped Italian flat leaf parsley

DIRECTIONS

1. Heavily salt a large pot of boiling water and add 1 lb. of ziti. Cook until al dente.

2. In a mixing bowl add Ricotta, 1/2 cup of grated Pecorino Romano cheese, about 5 oz. of mozzarella chopped into 1 inch cubes, 2 ladle fulls of homemade sauce (about 1 cup), plenty of cracked black pepper, and about 1 tsp. of kosher salt.

3. Mix the ingredients in the bowl. The result should be a pink color after mixing. If it's too white...add a little more sauce.

4. Then, add the cooked ziti into the bowl and mix all together.

5. In a casserole dish I used: 15.25 x 9.87 x 6.50 Inches (LxWxH) layer in this order: enough sauce to cover the bottom of the dish with a thin layer, half of the ziti mixture, cubed mozzarella, Pecorino Romano, cracked black pepper, fresh parsley, rest of the ziti mixture, more cubed up mozzarella, more grated Pecorino Romano, more sauce (about 2 ladle fulls) thick layer, rest of the cubed mozzarella, grated pecorino romano, cracked black pepper, and fresh chopped Italian salt leaf parsley.

6. Cover with foil and bake 30 minutes at 400 degrees F.; then uncover and bake another 30 minutes at 400 degrees F. or until browned and bubbly! (about 1 hour total cooking time)

7. Cool the baked ziti a 1/2 hour before serving! It will set up and become firmer!

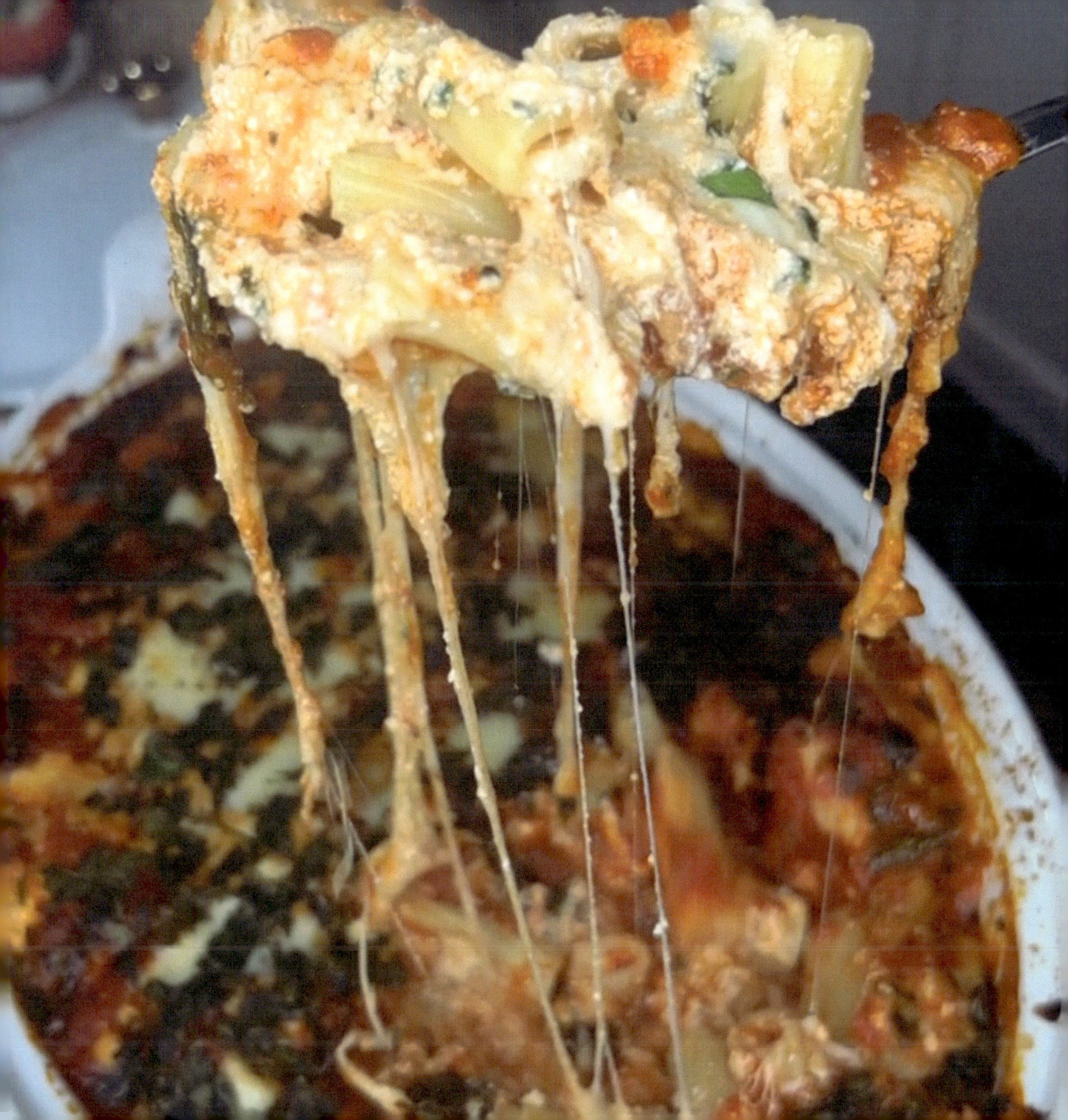

SUNDAY SAUCE

SERVES 8-10

INGREDIENTS

3-4 of pork shoulder country style ribs

3-4 Italian Sausage links I use hot Italian sausage

4-5 tbsp of extra virgin olive oil

28 oz can of San Marzano peeled tomatoes

2 (28 oz) cans of San Marzano crushed tomatoes

7-8 cloves of chopped garlic

a pinch of sugar about 1 tsp

1 can of tomato paste 6 oz

2 large handfuls of fresh basil about 4 oz

6 oz of red wine

crushed red pepper to taste about 1 tsp

Italian herbs to taste about 2 tbsp

garlic powder to taste about 2 tbsp

salt & pepper to taste about 2 tbsp

small hunk of Pecorino Romano cheese

2 bay leaves

water as needed about 12 oz

Grated Pecorino Romano cheese as much as you want to serve with

DIRECTIONS

1. Season the country style pork ribs with salt, pepper, and garlic powder (pork style ribs and sausage must be at room temperature before browning)
2. Add olive oil to a large pan with high sides and heat up at medium heat.
3. Add the sausage and pork style ribs and brown on all sides at medium heat.
4. Remove the sausage and ribs once they are browned and set aside on a plate (they won't be cooked all the way through yet)
5. Brown your meatballs in the same pot. Then, remove the meatballs and set aside.
6. At medium heat sauté crushed red pepper, black pepper, and salt, and fresh chopped garlic (this will only take a minute or so...don't burn the garlic!)
7. Deglaze pan with the red wine and allow the alcohol to cook out of it (about a couple minutes)
8. Add the peeled and crushed tomatoes to the pot along with Italian seasoning, garlic powder, salt, pepper, and a pinch of sugar. Bring the pot to a boil. Cover halfway and lower to a simmer and cook for about 20 minutes.
9. After 20 minutes, add both cans of crushed tomatoes and the tomato paste. Fill the small can of tomato paste with water twice and add to the pot. Bring to a boil.
10. Once the pot comes to a boil, lower and add a hunk of Pecorino Romano cheese and two bay leaves. Add the sausage, pork, and meatballs back into the pot. Bring back to a boil, then lower to a simmer and cover the pot halfway with the lid. Simmer slowly and low at least 2 hours up to 5 hours. (add water as needed throughout cooking process)
11. After about 30-40 minutes minutes of simmering TASTE THE SAUCE ... then add more seasonings as needed.
12. When the sauce is nearly complete add the fresh basil and cook 5 minutes more
13. Serve over your pasta of choice and drizzle a little olive oil over the dish then smother with grated pecorino Romano cheese.
14. Enjoy the BEST dinner EVER! Mangia! Mangia!

Farfalle

GRANDMAS JO'S MEATBALLS

SERVES 8

INGREDIENTS

1.5 lbs of ground chuck beef

½ cup Italian breadcrumbs

½ cup of Panko breadcrumbs

10-12 cloves of chopped garlic

2 eggs

⅓ cup of grated Pecorino Romano Cheese

½ tsp of crushed red pepper flakes

handful of fresh chopped basil

¼ cup of chopped fresh parsley

about 2 hunks of a loaf of a day old baguette. (Half the size of your hand)

about ¼ cup of milk

about 2 tsp of each: Kosher salt & cracked black pepper

3-4 tbsp of olive oil for frying

a pot of sauce for simmering

DIRECTIONS

1. In a large bowl add ground chuck (room temperature), breadcrumbs, garlic, eggs,

2. In a small cereal size bowl rip up a hunk of a day old baguette. cover in milk and soak for 15 minutes. Squeeze the milk out of the bread and add to the meatball mixture. (The baguette should be a damp moist consistency)

3. Mix everything together with your hands to incorporate, but don't over mix.

4. In the same pot you are making your sauce, brown the meatballs on all sides on medium heat in olive oil. Once they are lightly browned remove them from the pot and set aside on a plate or in a bowl.

5. Once you are ready to simmer the sauce, add the meatballs into the pot of sauce and simmer in the sauce for about 1-2 hours or until the sauce is done.

6. Enjoy!!

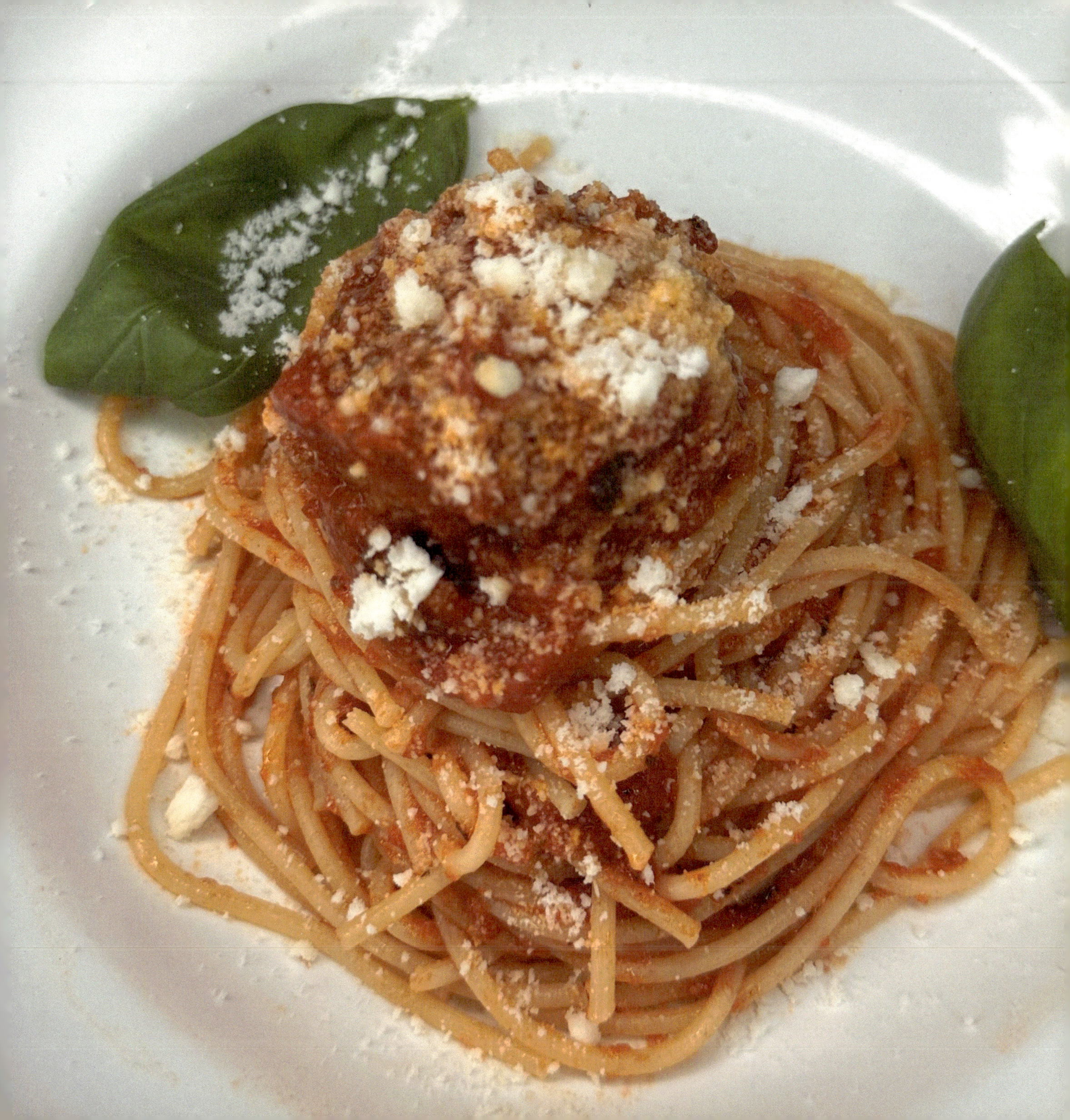

LASAGNA

SERVES 6-7

INGREDIENTS

1 lb of lasagna

Béchamel: 6 tbsp of all purpose flour, 6 tbsp of butter, 4 cups of milk, 1 tsp white pepper, 1 tsp salt, ½ tsp of nutmeg, & 3 oz of grated Parmigiano Reggiano

Homemade Ragu (meat) Sauce (about 2 qts)

2 cups of freshly shredded mozzarella

½ cup of freshly grated Pecorino Romano

Ricotta Balls: 16 oz Ricotta, 6 oz cubed fresh mozzarella, 1 egg, ¼ cup grated Pecorino Romano, ½ cup of fresh chopped parsley, handful of ripped up fresh basil, 1 tsp of salt & pepper

Top of lasagna garnish: fresh parsley & basil

DIRECTIONS

1. Béchamel: In a saucepan whisk together butter and flour continuously for about 5 minutes at medium-low heat. Then add room temperature milk 1 cup at a time. Whisk in intervals until it thickens and add another cup. Continue until it's all added and turns into a slightly thick sauce. Whisk continuously! Then add the seasonings and cheese and whisk until smooth and combined. Set aside.

2. Boil lasagna until 1 minute before the box indicates al dente. Then remove and separate.

3. Mix together the ingredients for the ricotta balls just until combined.

4. Start with adding enough Ragu or meat sauce to cover the bottom of a baking dish. I used a 9x13 baking dish. Then, add 3-4 sheets of lasagna. Cover the lasagna with béchamel sauce evenly. Using a small cookie scoop add about 12 small dollops of the ricotta balls. Then, sprinkle over fresh mozzarella & Pecorino Romano Cheese. Add more Ragu or meat sauce next. Then, keep repeating until the top! (I made 3 layers)

5. LAST LAYER: lasagna, bechamel, mozzarella, freshly grated Parmigiano Reggiano, parsley, & basil.

6. Bake at 375° F for about 1 hour. Cover the first half of baking time with foil. Rest 25 minutes before serving and ENJOY!

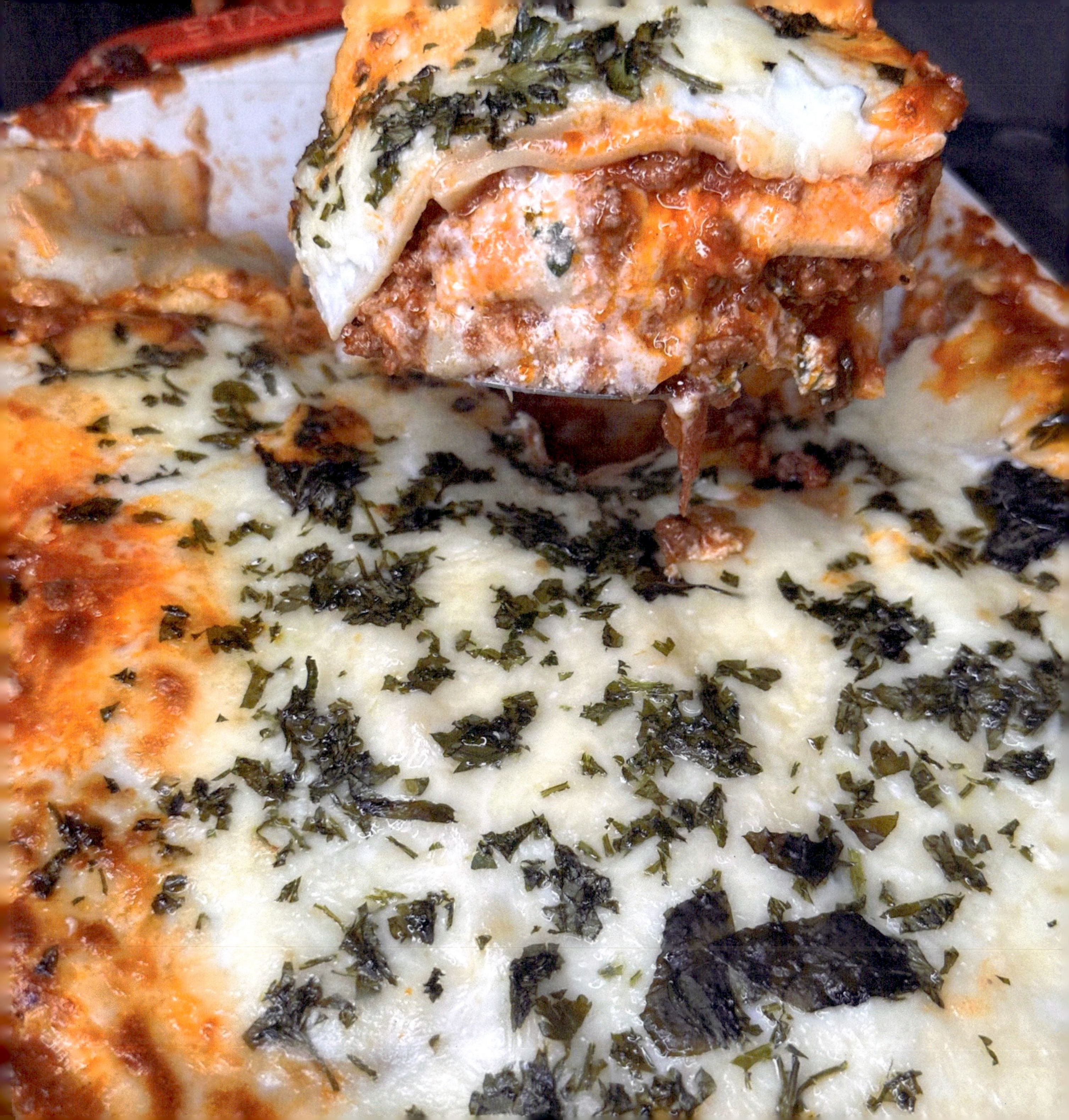

RAGU SAUCE

SERVES 8-10

INGREDIENTS

1 lb of ground pork

1 & ½ lbs of ground beef chuck

3 tbsp of olive oil

2 diced carrots

2 diced celery stalks

1 small diced onion

10 cloves of minced garlic

1 cup of Cabernet Sauvignon

35 oz can of whole peeled San Marzano tomatoes

24 oz jar of Passata (pureed tomatoes)

2 oz hunk of Parmigiano Reggiano

3 bay leaves

10 basil leaves ripped up

All seasonings to taste. Layer the seasonings throughout the cooking process. Start with 1 tsp of: salt, cracked black pepper, dried basil, dried oregano, crushed red pepper

DIRECTIONS

1. In a large dutch oven or soup pot; Sauté the carrots, celery, and onion in 3 tbsp of olive oil at medium-high heat. Season with salt, pepper, and crushed red pepper. Add the garlic once the veggies are translucent and sauté until fragrant.

2. Add the ground meat (season the meat with salt and pepper before adding) to the pot and sauté with the veggies until no longer pink.

3. If there's a lot of extra fat use tongs and a paper towel to remove some. BUT LEAVE some in!! Deglaze the pan with the red wine. Simmer for about 5 minutes.

4. Hand crush a can of San Marzano whole tomatoes and add into the sauce. Fill the can with 1/2 cup of water and swish around. Add to the sauce. Add a jar of Passata to the sauce. Fill the jar with another 1/2 cup of water and shake, add to the sauce.

5. Bring the pot to a boil & add the rest of the seasonings. Cut a hunk of Parmigiano Reggiano and add it into the pot.

6. Once boiling, lower to a simmer and cover the pot halfway with the lid. SImmer at least 30 minutes. Remove the lid and simmer for another 15 minutes. Add fresh basil at the last 5 minutes. Taste for seasoning. Add more if needed. BEST! Make IT!

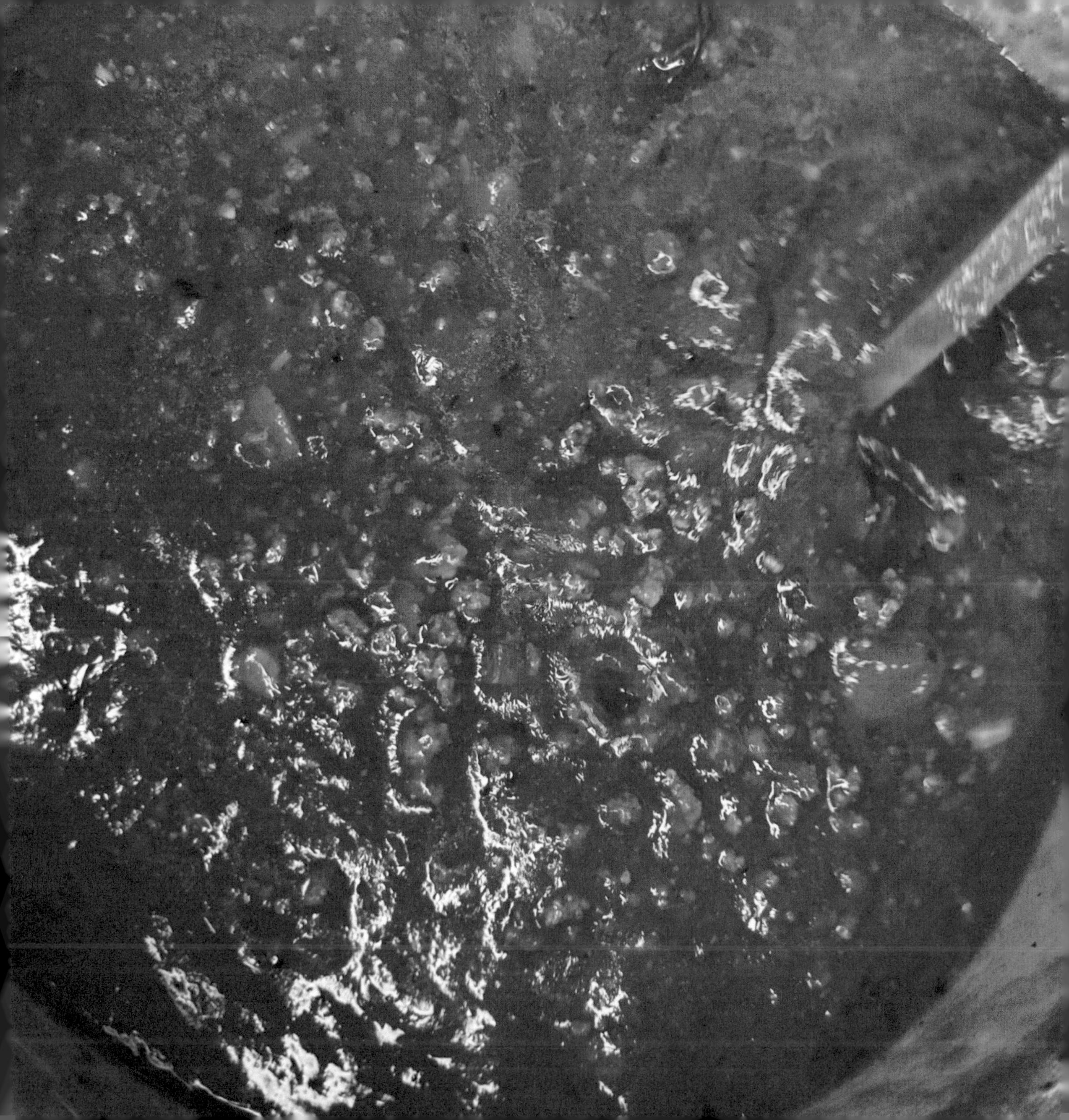

LASAGNA SOUP

SERVES 8-10

INGREDIENTS

1 tbsp olive oil

1 lb lasagna pasta broken in thirds

1.5 lbs ground beef

1 yellow onion chopped

6 cloves chopped garlic

2 tbsp tomato paste

2 tsp. of each: dried basil, parsley, oregano, Italian seasoning blend

(salt, cracked black pepper and crushed red pepper to taste)

28 oz. can of crushed tomatoes

6 & ½ cups of chicken broth

1 cup of heavy cream

handful of fresh basil

Cheese Balls: 15 oz. ricotta, 1 cup of shredded mozzarella, ½ cup of grated Pecorino or parmesan cheese, ¼ cup of chopped fresh curly parsley, tsp. of salt, tsp of black pepper

DIRECTIONS

1. In a dutch oven or soup pot, brown up ground beef and onions with olive oil.
2. Once the beef is nearly cooked through, add the garlic and sauté together.
3. Add the tomato paste and brown it up for a couple minutes. Add all of the seasonings: mix and sauté.
4. Add a can of crushed tomatoes, chicken stock, & heavy cream. Cover and bring to a boil.
5. Uncover once boiling and add the lasagna in the pot. Boil uncovered until the lasagna is al dente.
6. Add fresh basil and simmer at low heat.
7. Mix together the ricotta, mozzarella, parsley, grated parmesan, salt, and pepper. Roll into balls.
8. Turn the heat off and add the cheese balls immediately into the soup. Allow the residual heat to melt the balls until gooey and soft but still keep their shape.
9. Serve up the best soup ever! Make IT!

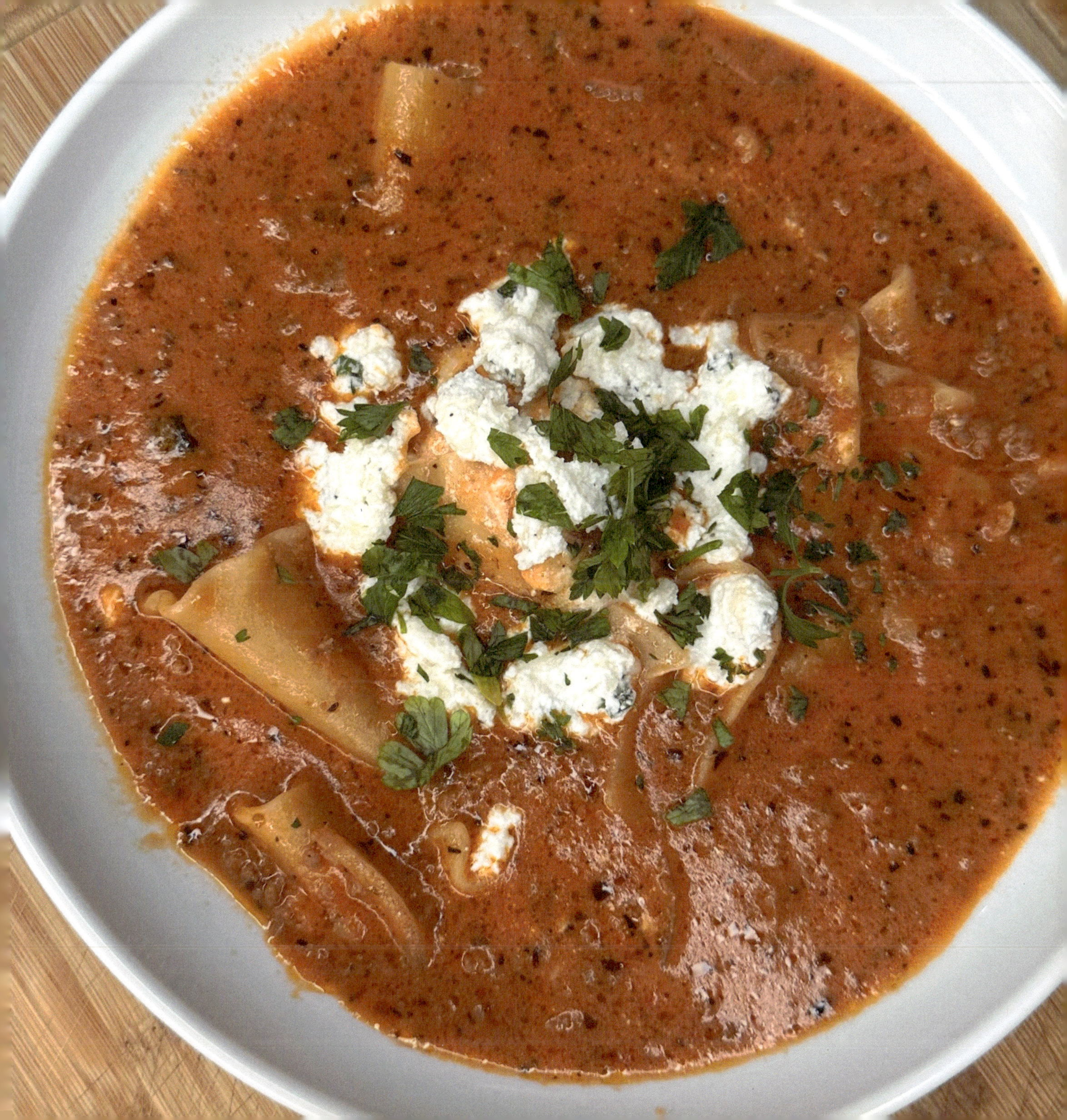

RIGATONI ALLA VODKA

SERVES 6

INGREDIENTS

1 lb rigatoni pasta

1 cup heavy cream

6 oz can tomato paste

½ cup pecorino romano

½ a medium onion, chopped finely

6 cloves garlic, chopped finely

1-2 tbsp olive oil

2 tbsp butter

1 tsp crushed red pepper

2 oz vodka

¼ + 1 cup of pasta water, divided

Salt and pepper to taste

DIRECTIONS

1. Boil a large pot of water, salt it generously.
2. In a pan with high sides add onion, garlic, red pepper flakes, salt & pepper, and sauté in butter and olive oil until translucent.
3. Tempered cream: once the water is reaching a boil in the large pot scoop out about 1/4 cup of water and add to the heavy cream and stir (set this aside until you need it)
4. Once water is boiling add in your rigatoni pasta.
5. To the pan add the tomato paste and sauté about 5 minutes on medium heat.
6. Add the vodka and let the alcohol burn out at least one minute or so before adding other ingredients.
7. Reduce the heat to medium-low and add the tempered cream (stir until combined and pink).
8. Set aside 1 cup of pasta water.
9. Once the rigatoni is al dente add pasta to the pan and start adding the reserved pasta water until the sauce reaches the consistency you desire.
10. Add the Pecorino Romano and take the pan off the heat and stir it in.
11. Garnish with fresh basil and more pecorino Romano cheese. Enjoy!!!

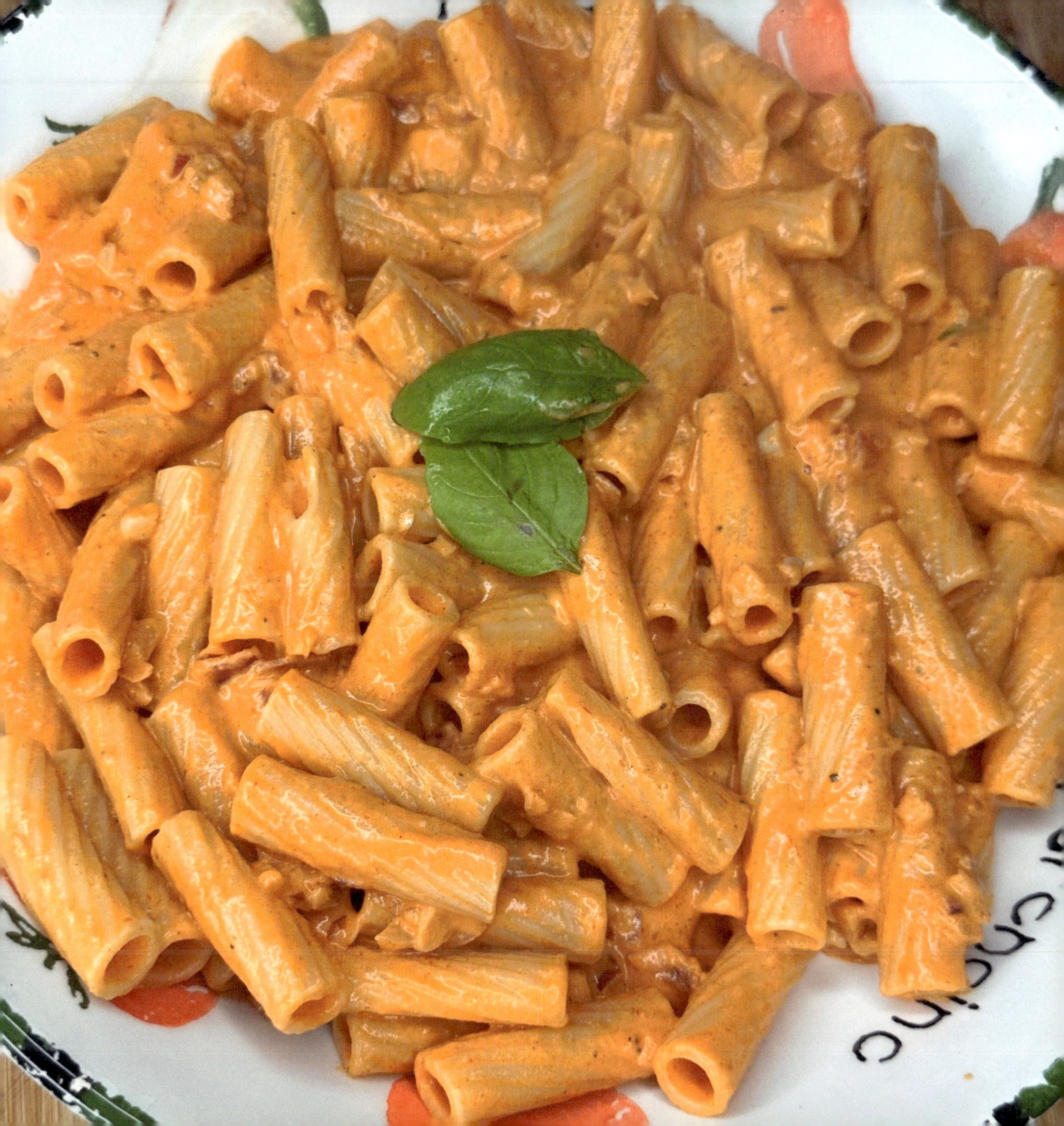

CHRISTMAS EVE SHRIMP LINGUINE

SERVES 10

INGREDIENTS

2 lbs of extra large shrimp peeled, deveined, and tails off

2 lbs of linguine

2 pints of white mushrooms, sliced

2-3 tbsp of olive oil

3 tbsp of butter

1 large chopped sweet onion

8-10 cloves of minced garlic

1 pint of cherry tomatoes, halved

14 oz can of artichoke hearts, drained and chopped

8 oz. black olives, rough chop

Juice of half a lemon

6 oz of white wine

Handful of fresh basil, chopped

Handful of fresh parsley, chopped

1 tbsp garlic powder

Salt & pepper to taste

½ - 1 cup of pasta water

Crushed red pepper flakes, as spicy as you want

DIRECTIONS

1. Peel your shrimp and pat dry; in a large pan add olive oil, butter, shrimp, salt & pepper, and sauté on medium to high heat until shrimp are pink.

2. In a large pot bring water to a boil, salt your water, and add in the linguine.

3. Once the shrimp are pink, remove from the pan and set aside. In that same pan add more butter and oil, and add in onion, crushed red pepper, minced garlic, cherry tomatoes, artichoke hearts, black olives, and sauté on medium heat.

4. Deglaze the pan with white wine, juice of half a lemon, and add in garlic powder, basil, parsley, and mix together; then add shrimp back in and all the juices.

5. In a separate pan add oil, butter, mushrooms, salt & pepper, and sauté until soft, once soft drain them.

6. In a large tray add in cooked pasta, shrimp mixture, mushrooms, and some pasta water; mix everything together, and top with more fresh parsley. Enjoy!!

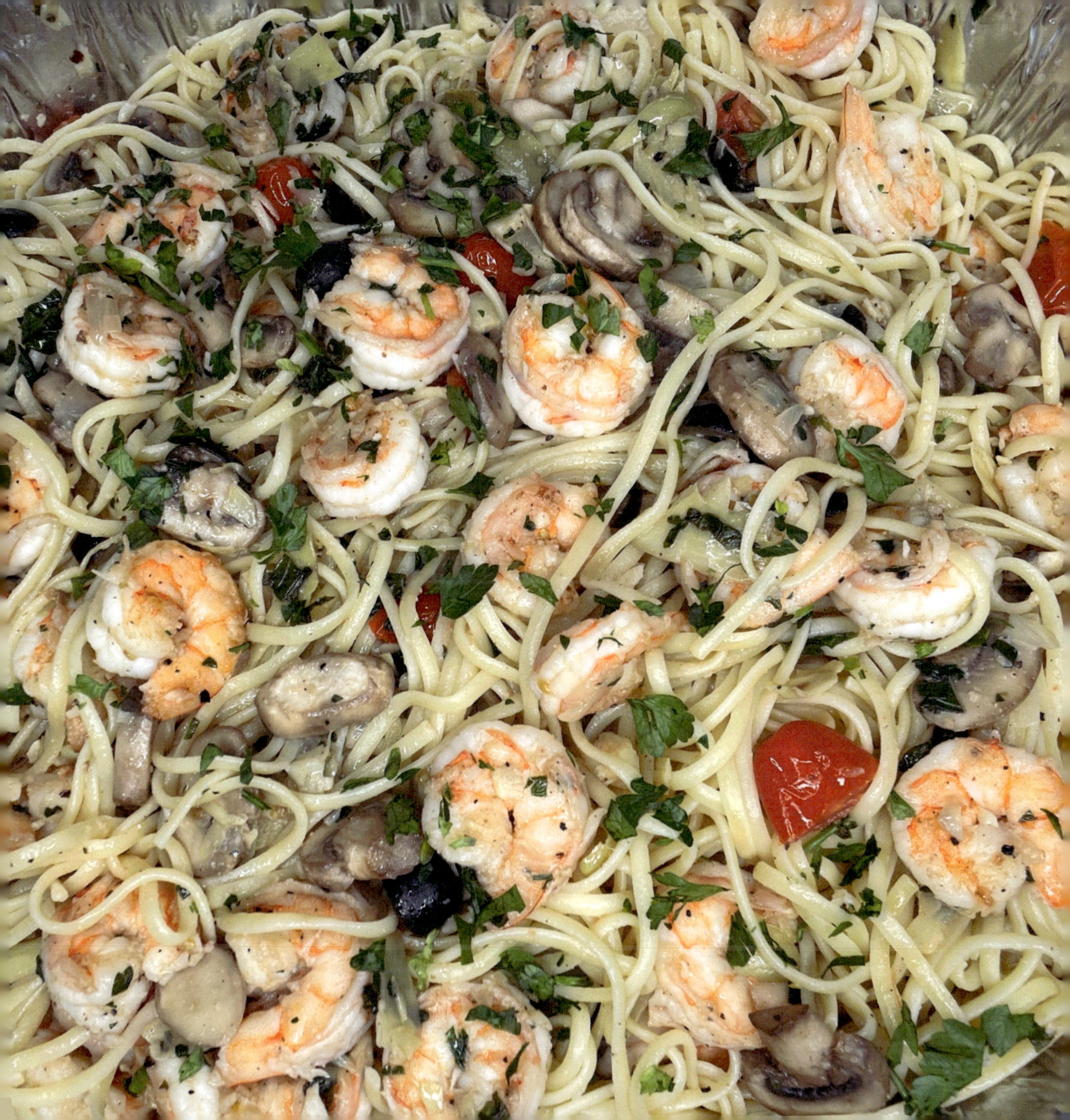

SHRIMP SCAMPI

SERVES 6

INGREDIENTS

1 lb shell on, deveined frozen shrimp

1 & ½ cups of white wine

3 tbsp worcestershire, divided

8 garlic cloves chopped + 5 cloves whole

1 bunch of parsley, divided

1 lemon

Salt & pepper to taste

1 tsp Old Bay seasoning

1 shallot, chopped

1 tsp crushed red pepper

1 tsp of calabrian chili oil

6-7 tbsp olive oil, divided

6-7 tbsp of butter

Cornstarch slurry: 1 tbsp cornstarch + juice of ½ lemon

¾ of a pound of thin spaghetti

DIRECTIONS

1. In a bowl separate the deveined shrimp from the shells, set the shells aside.
2. Pat dry & season the shrimp with old bay seasoning, salt & pepper, and let that marinate for 30 minutes.
3. For the broth: in a pan with high sides, cover the bottom with olive oil, add your shrimp shells, salt & pepper, 1 tbsp worcestershire, about 4 sprigs of parsley , 5 whole garlic cloves, and sauté on medium heat for a about 10 minutes. or until fragrant & pink.
4. To the same pan add white wine, the juice of a lemon, and bring it to a boil then drop it to a simmer. Cook for 10 minutes then strain all of the juice out, saving the broth.
5. Wipe out the pan & cover the bottom with olive oil, Calabrian chili oil, chopped shallot, chopped garlic, crushed red pepper, zest of a lemon, and sauté until translucent. Then deglaze with 2 tbsp of worcestershire, add 3 tbsp of chopped parsley, 4 hunks of butter, and shrimp, sauté on medium to high heat.
6. In a large pot bring water to a boil, heavily salt it, and boil your thin spaghetti until 2 minutes before the box indicates it is done.
7. Once the shrimp are pink, add in the broth and cornstarch slurry (A mix of 1 tbsp cornstarch & juice of half a lemon). Simmer for about 5 minutes until it thickens and reduces. Add the pasta to the pan and let some of the pasta water drip in, simmer for about 5 minutes together. finish it off with two hunks of butter and more chopped parsley. Enjoy!

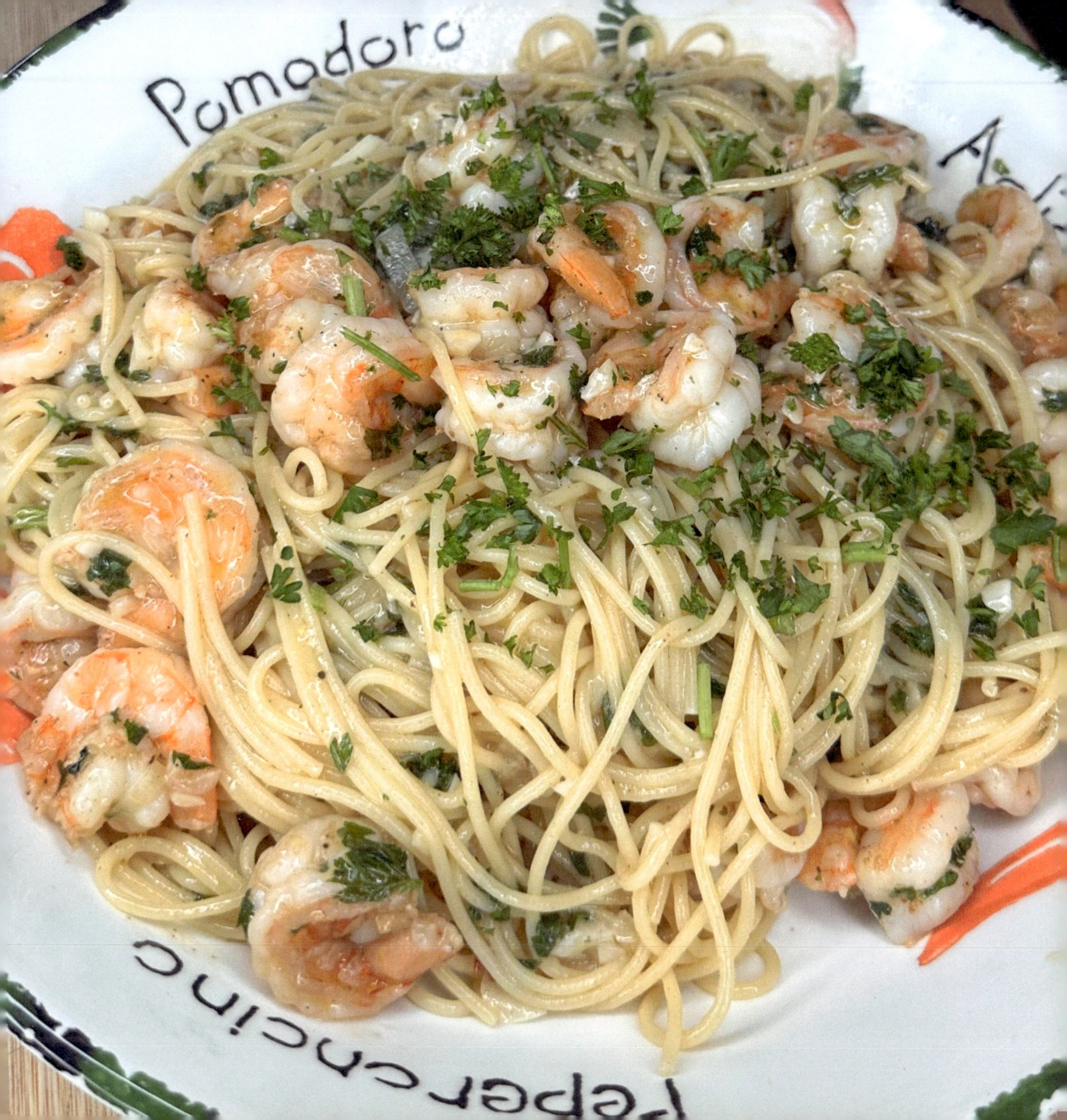
Pomodoro

LINGUINE & CLAMS

SERVES 6

INGREDIENTS

¼ cup + 2 tbsp extra virgin olive oil

1 tsp. Calabrian Chili Oil

1 stick salted butter divided

16 oz raw chopped sea clams (drained)

1 lb linguine

1 cup of Italian White Wine

1 cup of clam juice

¾ cups of pasta water

1 tsp of oregano flakes

¼ tsp crushed red pepper flakes

¼ cup of chopped fresh parsley

7-8 cloves of chopped garlic

salt & cracked black pepper to taste

1 oz of fresh basil

Garnish: Pecorino Romano, fresh parsley and basil

DIRECTIONS

1. In a skillet with high sides heat up olive oil and Calabrian chili oil at medium heat. Start boiling linguini in a pot of heavily salted water.

2. Sauté the garlic, parsley, oregano, chili flakes, salt, pepper, and 1/2 stick of butter. Once fragrant & golden deglaze with a cup or so of white wine. Simmer for a few minutes.

3. Add the clam juice and simmer for another 3-5 minutes. Add the clams into the skillet. They get tough if cooked too long. They only take 2-3 minutes. So, add a couple minutes before the pasta is ready to go in.

4. Add in another 2 tbsp. of olive oil & fresh basil

5. Remove the linguini from the boiling water 2 minutes before the box indicates. Add it into the skillet. Toss together. add 4 tbsp of butter on top of the linguini and let it melt in. Simmer 2-3 minutes. Serve, garnish, and enjoy!

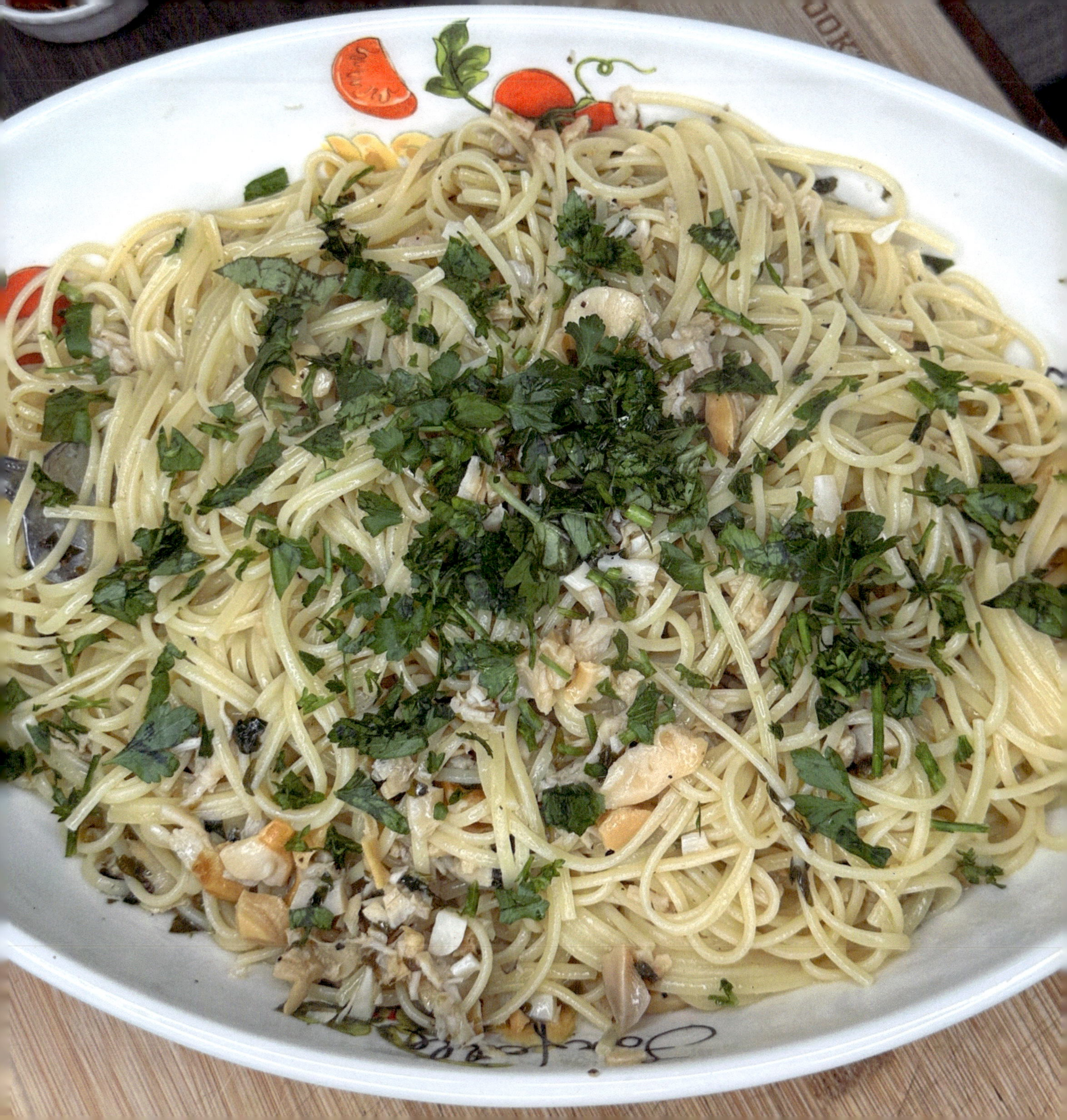

PASTA FAGIOLI

SERVES 6-8

INGREDIENTS

6 slices of bacon, chopped

1 onion, chopped

28 oz can of San Marzano whole peeled tomatoes

8 garlic cloves, chopped

Salt & pepper to taste, must layer as you go

Shake of crushed red pepper to taste

1 tbsp of garlic powder to taste

4 tbsp flour

Water; fill 28 oz can with water + 6 more cups

3 cans of cannellini beans, drained & rinsed

3 oz hunk of Pecorino Romano

2 bay leaves

1 lb of ditalini pasta

about 3 tbsp of olive oil

A handful of basil, ripped up

For garnish: Drizzle of extra virgin olive oil and freshly grated Pecorino Romano

DIRECTIONS

1. In a large pot, add chopped bacon and render the fat on medium heat for about 5 minutes.
2. In a bowl add peeled tomatoes and crush them with your hands, set aside.
3. In the pot add in chopped onion, garlic, crushed red pepper, garlic powder, salt & pepper, olive oil, and sauté until the bacon is, NOT crisp...just until it's golden and fatty.
4. Then shake over your flour and whisk continuously for 3-4 minutes.
5. Fill the 28 oz tomato can with water and add into the pot, whisk again for about 5 minutes on medium to high heat.
6. Bring the pot to a boil, add in 1 can of drained rinsed cannellini beans and mash then up in the pot using a potato masher until crushed but not pureed.
7. Then add in crushed tomatoes, 6 cups of water, Pecorino Romano hunk, bay leaves, and let it boil uncovered for about 30 minutes.
8. Layer with salt & pepper as you go to taste
9. Once the soup reduces in the pot about 1/4 of the way down, add in 2 cans of drained rinsed cannellini beans and ditalini pasta; boil until the ditalini is al dente, about 11 minutes.
10. Once you take it off the burner, while it's still hot, add in ripped basil and stir together.
11. When serving garnish with grated Pecorino Romano and extra virgin olive oil. Enjoy!

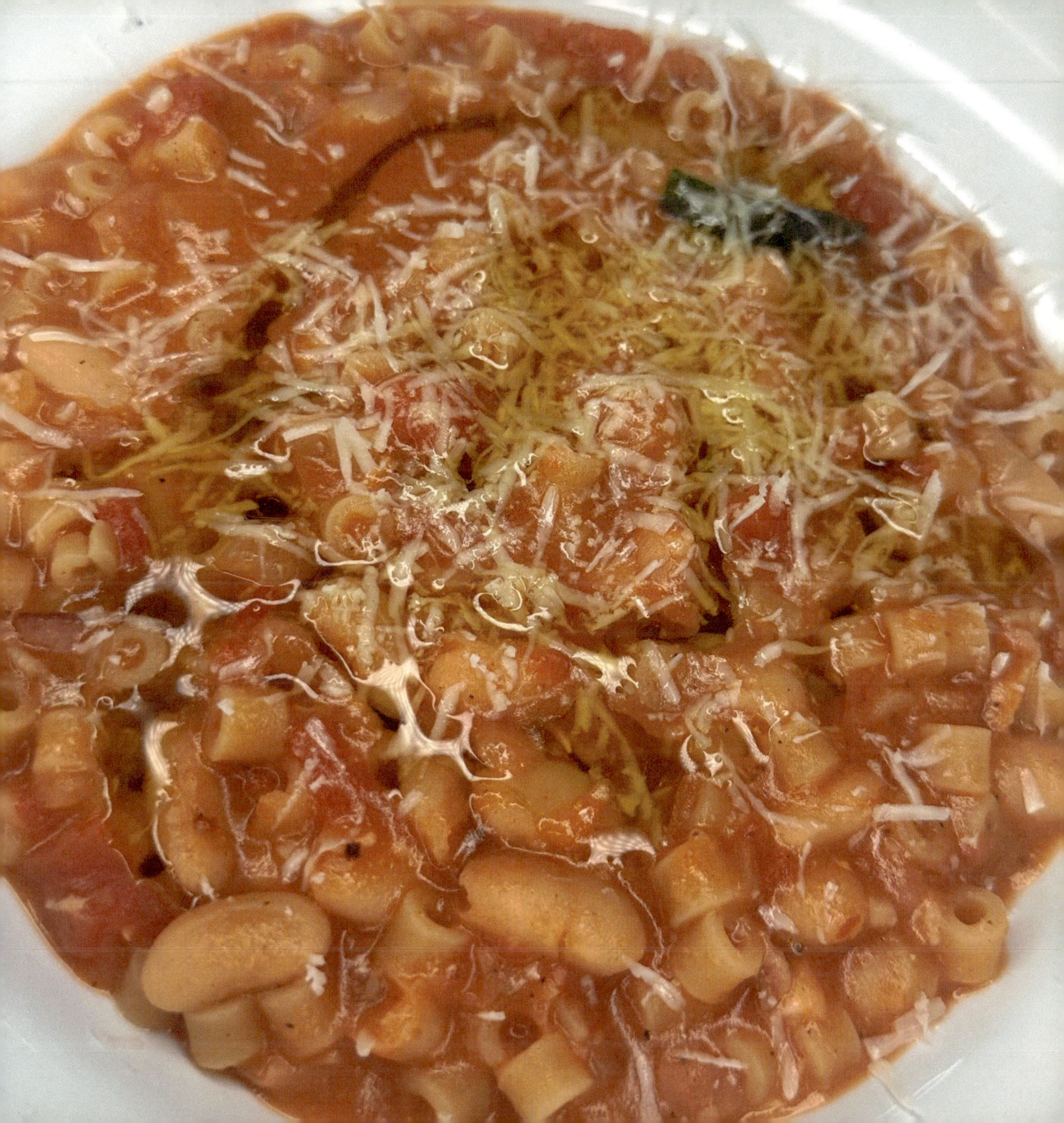

BACON CARBONARA

SERVES 6

INGREDIENTS

6 pieces of bacon, chopped

1 lb of linguine pasta

5 eggs (2 whole & 3 yolks)

4 oz Pecorino Romano hunk, divided

6-7 cloves garlic, chopped

¾ cup pasta water

¼ cup chopped fresh parsley, divided

1-2 tbsp of olive oil

About 2 tbsp of cracked black pepper (to taste)

DIRECTIONS

1. Your timing needs to be right so first start by bringing a pot of water to boil.
2. Chop your bacon into pieces and add them into a pan on medium heat with about 1-2 tbsp of olive oil. The goal is to get the bacon crisp but still fatty.
3. In a bowl add in 2 whole egg.s and just the yolks of 3 eggs and whisk it together
4. In the same bowl grate in about 3 oz of a hunk of Pecorino Romano & add cracked black pepper. Whisk everything together and set aside.
5. Once the bacon is almost done add garlic and cracked black pepper to the pan. Sauté together for a few minutes then set it aside off the heat to wait for the pasta.
6. Once water is boiling, salt it, and add the linguine. Cook pasta until al dente.
7. Once the pasta is al dente make sure the pan with the bacon is at medium-low heat and begin adding the pasta to the pan with about 3/4 cup of the pasta water. Stir together and incorporate.
8. Next turn the pan off, immediately add the eggs and cheese mixture, and stir quickly and consistently to make the cream sauce.
9. Add in some cracked black pepper and fresh parsley and mix it in.
10. To serve garnish with more freshly grated pecorino romano and parsley. Enjoy!!!

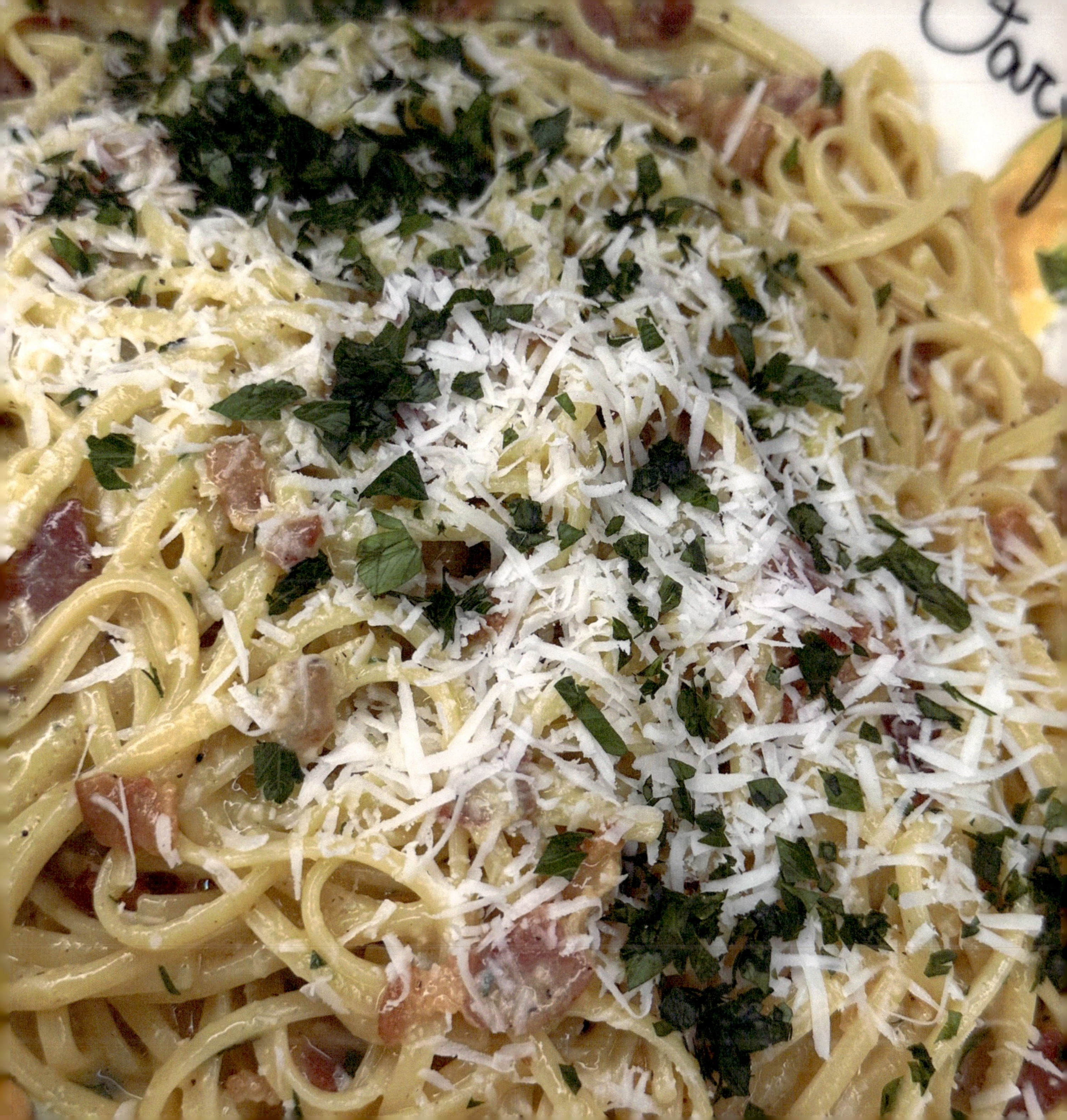

GRANDMAS ARTICHOKE QUICHE

SERVES 6-8

INGREDIENTS

2 (14 oz) cans of quartered artichoke hearts

3-4 cloves of minced garlic

1 tbsp. of butter

1 tbsp. of olive oil

4 eggs

¾ cup of heavy cream

2 cups of mozzarella cut into little cubes ½ inch cubes Polly-O whole milk mozzarella is my favorite for this dish.

¼ cup of grated Pecorino Romano cheese

One Deep Dish Pillsbury Pie Crust from frozen section

Salt & cracked black pepper to taste start with at least 1 tsp of each

DIRECTIONS

1. Drain both cans of artichoke hearts and squeeze all of the moisture out. Then roughly chop the artichoke hearts. (not too small)

2. In a pan at medium heat saute the artichoke hearts, chopped garlic, salt, pepper, and crushed red pepper in butter and olive oil until fragrant and incorporated. (about 5-7 minutes)

3. In a bowl add 4 room temperature eggs and heavy cream. Whisk until incorporated. Then whisk in the grated Pecorino Romano Cheese.

4. Chop up a block of mozzarella into little cubes.

5. Fold in the mozzarella and add another pinch of salt & pepper.

6. Pour the mixture into a deep dish Pillsbury pie plate. Bake at 350 degrees F for 50-60 minutes.

7. Allow quiche to rest a half hour before slicing. Serve warm or cold! Make it!

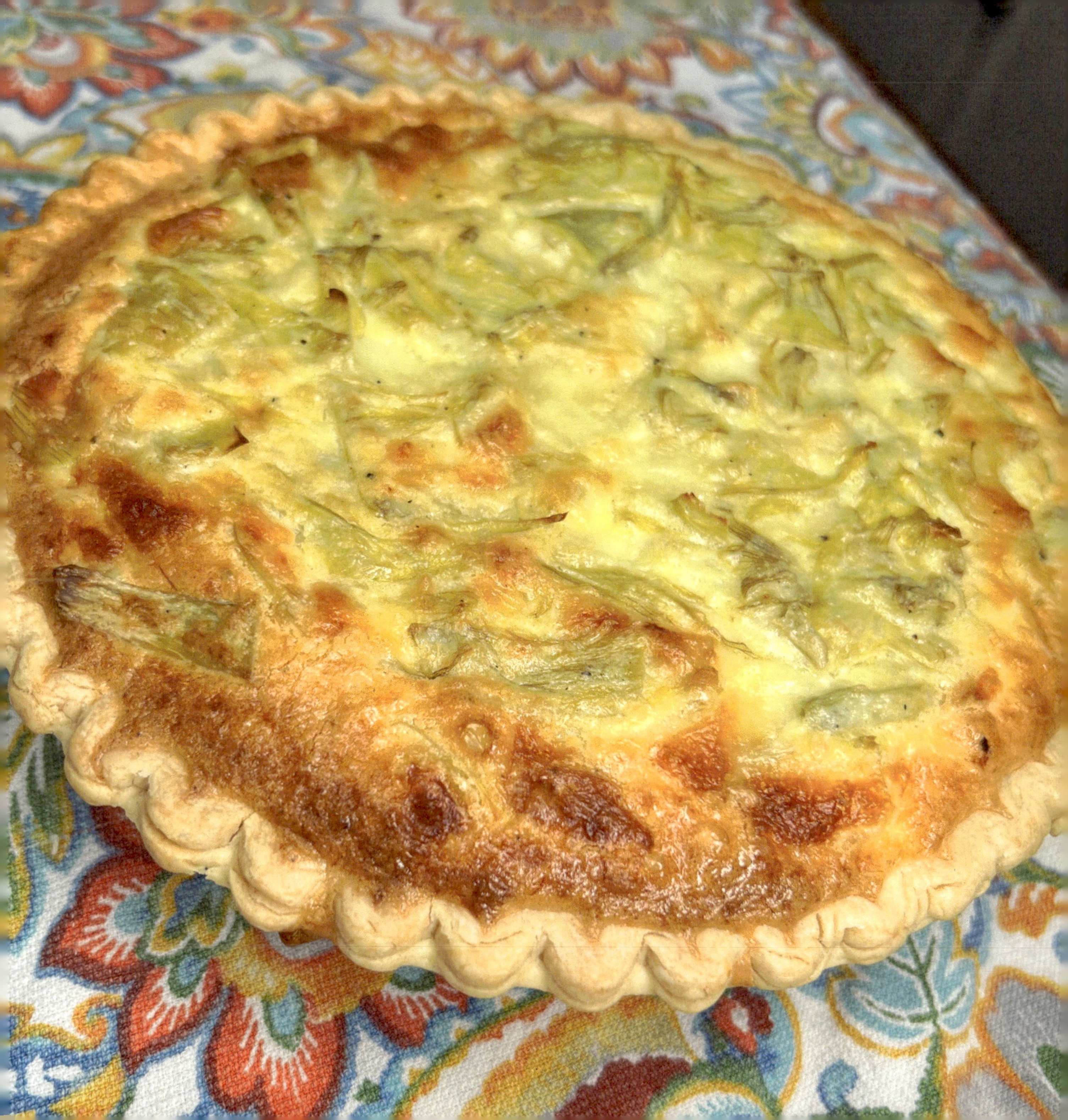

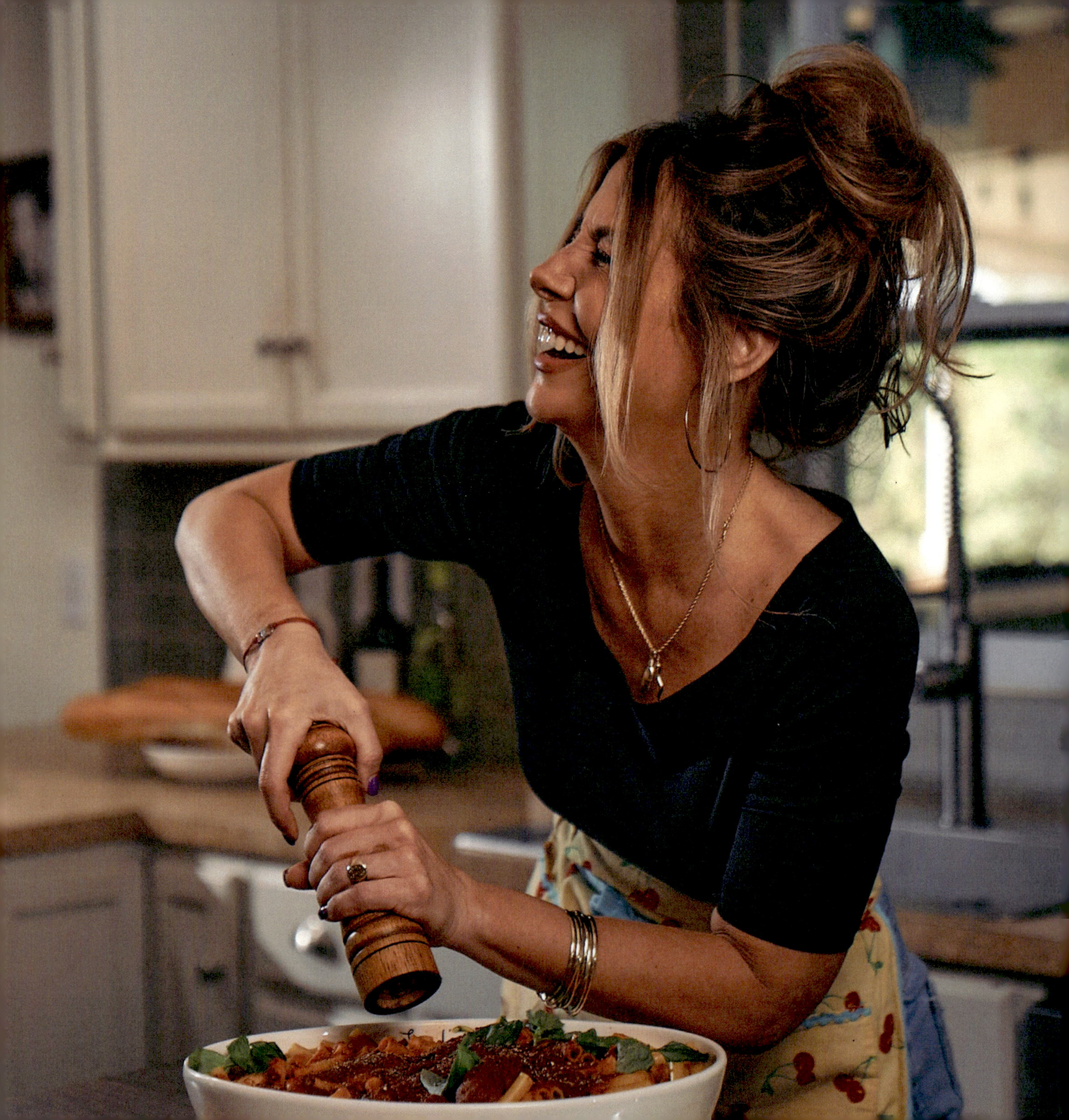

One Pot Meals & Soups

CHICKEN POT PIE SOUP

SERVES 8-10

INGREDIENTS

3 chicken breasts, shredded

2 chicken bouillon cubes

2 carrots, sliced & peeled

4 stalks of celery with some of the leaves, chopped

2 potatoes, peeled & chopped

7-8 garlic cloves, chopped

1 medium onion, chopped

8 tbsp of butter, divided

1 tbsp of neutral oil

Salt & pepper

1 tbsp chicken bouillon seasoning

1 tsp: Slap Yo Mama seasoning & garlic powder

8 cups of reserved chicken broth

1 cup heavy cream

½ cup + 2 tbsp of flour

7.5 oz frozen peas

¼ cup chopped parsley

16.3 oz pack of Pillsbury Grands original biscuits

2 tbsp honey

DIRECTIONS

1. In a pot of water boil 3 chicken breasts on a rolling boil for about 3 minutes then lower to a simmer, add 2 chicken bouillon cubes, once chicken is cooked, shred it, and save broth it's going to be used as the broth.

2. In a separate pot add 6 tbsp butter, oil, sliced carrots, celery with some of the leaves chopped, onion, salt & pepper (layer the salt and pepper as you go), chicken bouillon seasoning, Slap Yo Mama seasoning, and sauté together about 5 minutes on medium to high heat

3. Then add in chopped garlic and garlic powder, sauté a few more minutes.

4. Add 1/2 cup + 2 tbsp of flour to the veggie mixture and whisk continuously for about 5 minutes.

5. Add in your reserved broth and whisk for a few minutes, then add your chopped potatoes.

6. Add your heavy cream, stir, and bring the pot to a boil.

7. Add your frozen peas and shredded chicken, once it starts to boil, cover the pot with a lid about 3/4 of the way, lower it to a simmer and let it cook together for about 20-30 minutes or until potatoes are soft.

8. For the honey butter mix 2 tbsp of melted butter and honey, brush over the uncooked biscuits.

9. When the potatoes are soft, cut the heat, add chopped parsley, and taste to check if you need more seasonings. Lay biscuits evenly over the soup, transfer pot to the oven, and bake at 350° for 13-14 minutes. Make it!!

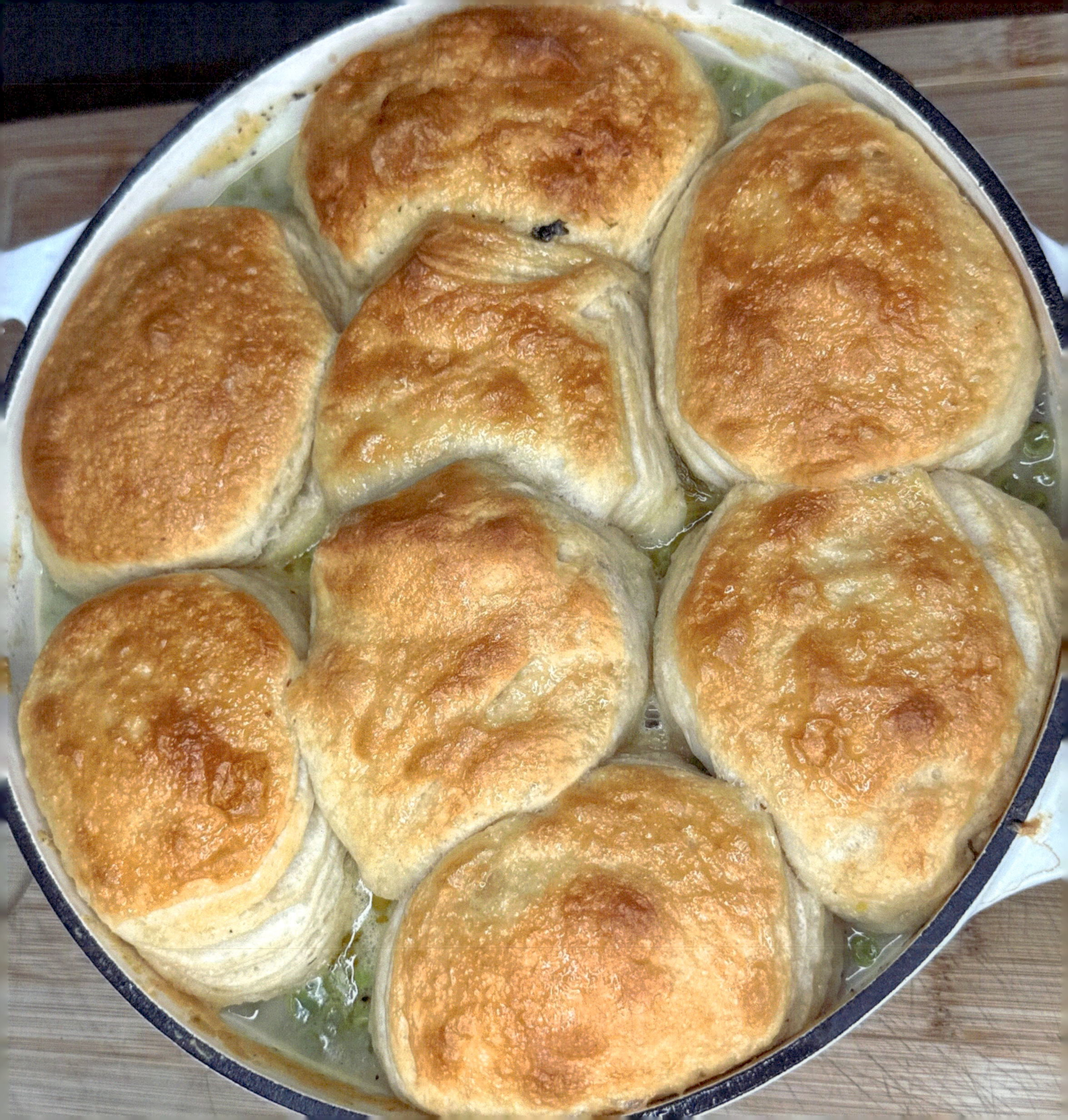

MARRY ME CHICKEN SOUP

SERVES 8

INGREDIENTS

2 large chicken breasts, shredded

2 chicken bouillon cubes

4 oz of diced pancetta (rendered fat and pancetta)

½ stick of butter (4 tbsp)

7-8 garlic cloves, chopped

1 medium onion, chopped

6 oz of chardonnay white wine

½ cup of all purpose flour

6 cups reserved chicken stock

1 quart of heavy cream

5 oz of sun-dried tomatoes sliced

10 oz. of cheese tortellini

¼ cup chopped parsley, handful of fresh basil, and 2 cups of baby spinach

½ cup of grated parmesan

Spices: 2 tsp of each: garlic powder, Italian seasoning blend, black pepper

1 tsp of each: salt, smoked paprika

DIRECTIONS

1. In a pot of water boil 2 chicken breasts on a rolling boil for about 3 minutes then lower to a simmer, add 2 chicken bouillon cubes, once chicken is cooked, shred it, and save the broth; it's going in the soup.

2. In a separate dutch oven add the pancetta and cook at medium heat until crisp but slightly fatty. Add butter, garlic, onions, and spices. Sauté at medium heat for 5-7 minutes or until golden.

3. Deglaze the pot with white wine and cook for about 5 minutes at medium.

4. Add 1/2 cup of flour and whisk continuously for about 3-5 minutes.

5. Add the reserved chicken stock and whisk another 2-3 minutes or until smooth. Add the heavy cream and sun-dried tomatoes; simmer for 5-7 minutes or until thickened.

6. Bring the pot to a boil and add the tortellini. Boil for 2-3 minutes. Add the fresh herbs, spinach, shredded chicken, & parmesan cheese. Simmer together until the tortellini is al dente. About 2-3 minutes.

7. Serve it up and enjoy!! Make it!!

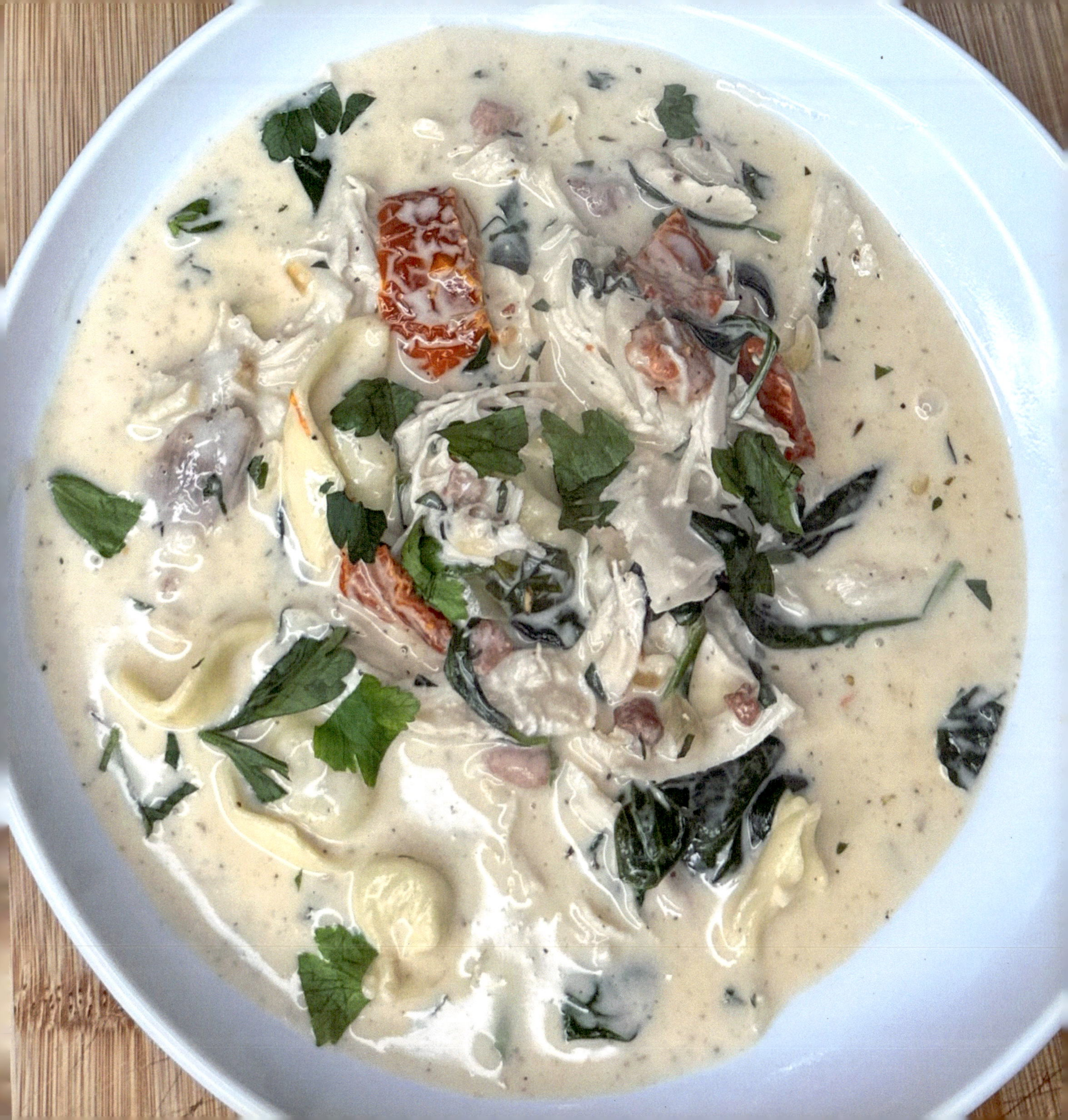

ONE POT CHICKEN PAPRIKA

SERVES 5

INGREDIENTS

4-5 bone in skin on chicken thighs

½ a small red onion, chopped

3-4 stalks green onion, chopped

2 stalks celery, chopped

½ a yellow bell pepper, chopped

7 cloves garlic, chopped

1 tbsp tomato paste

1 heaping tsp chicken base

1 cup long grain rice

1 & ½ cups of water

1 tbsp olive oil

2 tbsp butter

2 tbsp paprika

1 tbsp smoked paprika and dried parsley

1 tsp Italian seasoning

Kosher salt & pepper to taste (start with 2 tsp of each)

DIRECTIONS

1. Season room temperature, patted dry chicken thighs with paprika, smoked paprika, dried parsley, salt & pepper, and rub it into both sides and under the skin.

2. In a pan with oil and butter add in chicken thighs, brown on both sides.

3. Once chicken is browned on both sides, remove from the pan, and in the same pan add chopped onion, yellow bell pepper, celery, green onion, garlic, Italian seasoning, salt & pepper, and sauté for a few minutes on medium to high heat.

4. Add tomato paste and brown it for a few minutes.

5. Next add in chicken base and brown for a few minutes.

6. Add in long grain rice and sauté for a few more minutes.

7. Then add the water and put the chicken back in the pan with all the juices, bring it to a boil, and once it comes to a boil cover it with the lid.

8. Bake at 400°F for 40 minutes. Make it!!!

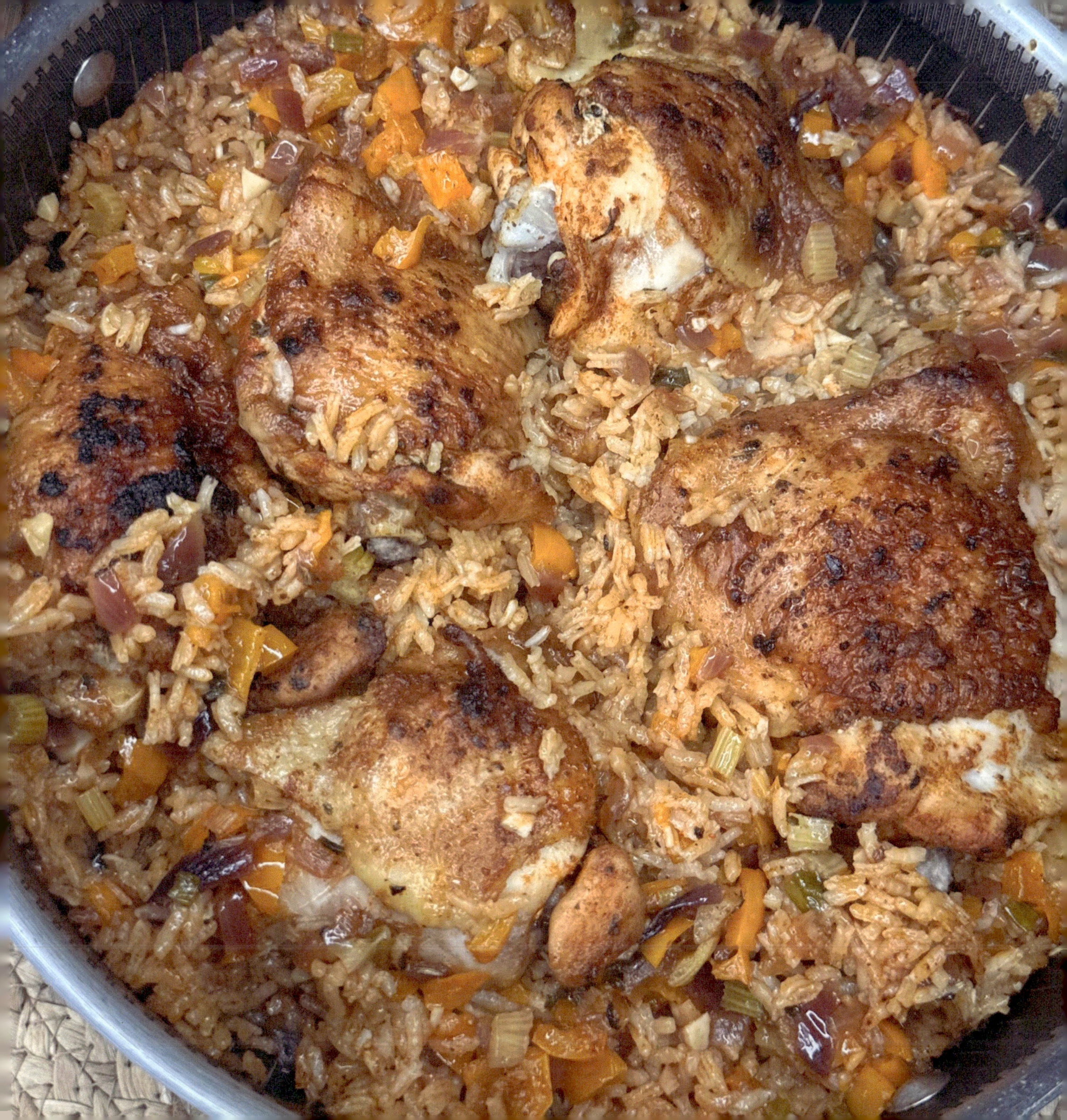

ONE POT CHICKEN & DIRTY RICE

SERVES 5

INGREDIENTS

7 oz smoked sausage

4 skin on bones in chicken thighs

½ tbsp: Tonys Creole & Slap Yo Mamma seasoning

1 tsp: smoked paprika, garlic powder, & onion powder

1 tbsp Italian seasoning

Salt & pepper

2 stalks of celery, chopped

1 small onion, chopped

Half of a bell pepper, chopped

5-6 garlic cloves, chopped

2 tbsp tomato paste

2 tsp chicken base

4 oz of white wine

Juice of 1 lemon

1 cup long grain rice

1 & ½ cups water

A couple shakes of Louisiana hot sauce

DIRECTIONS

1. Slice smoked sausage on the diagonal! (I used half of my sausage link pictured)
2. Brown sausage on each side in a little olive oil then remove from the pan.
3. Season chicken thighs with Tony's Creole, smoked paprika, onion & garlic powder, and Italian seasoning. Brown in the same pan (you aren't cooking through; just browning). About 5 minutes east side. Then remove to a plate.
4. In SAME PAN add chopped celery, onion, bell pepper, and sauté until golden (mop up some of the oil).
5. Then, add chopped garlic and sauté another minute or until golden.
6. Add & sauté tomato paste for a minute or so. Then add in chicken base and sauté another minute.
7. Deglaze with white wine and let alcohol burn out for a couple minutes.
8. Add lemon juice, Slap Ya momma seasoning, a couple shakes of Louisiana hot sauce, and salt & pepper!
9. Add rice and sauté a couple minutes, then add in water, and bring to boil. Once it's boiling lower to a simmer.
10. Nestle in the sausage and add the chicken on top with all its juices. Cover with the lid and bake in the oven at 400°F for about 40 minutes! Enjoy!

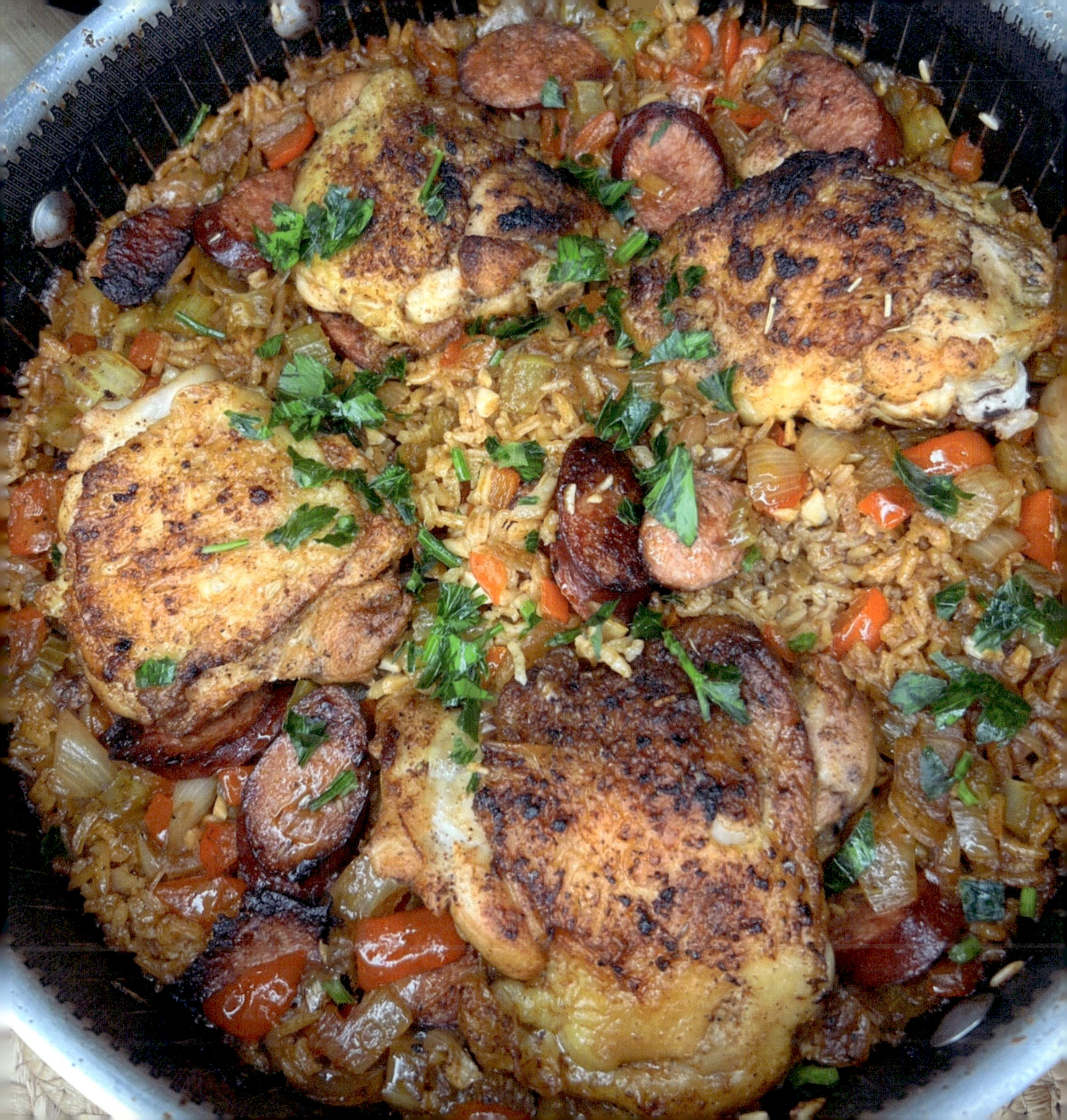

MISSISSIPPI CROCK POT ROAST

SERVES 6-7

INGREDIENTS

2.20 lb chuck roast

1 oz Au Jus Gravy packet

1 oz Hidden Valley Ranch seasoning packet

1 stick salted butter, cubed

8 oz Mezzetta medium heat sliced golden greek pepperoncinis with the juice

DIRECTIONS

1. In a crockpot add in your chuck roast.
2. Over the chuck roast sprinkle in a packet of Au Jus Gravy and a packet of Hidden Valley Ranch Seasoning.
3. Add in cubed butter on top.
4. Pour in about 8 oz of pepperoncinis with the juice
5. Then put on the lid and cook on low for 8 hours or on high for 6 hours.
6. Serve over mashed potatoes. Enjoy!!!

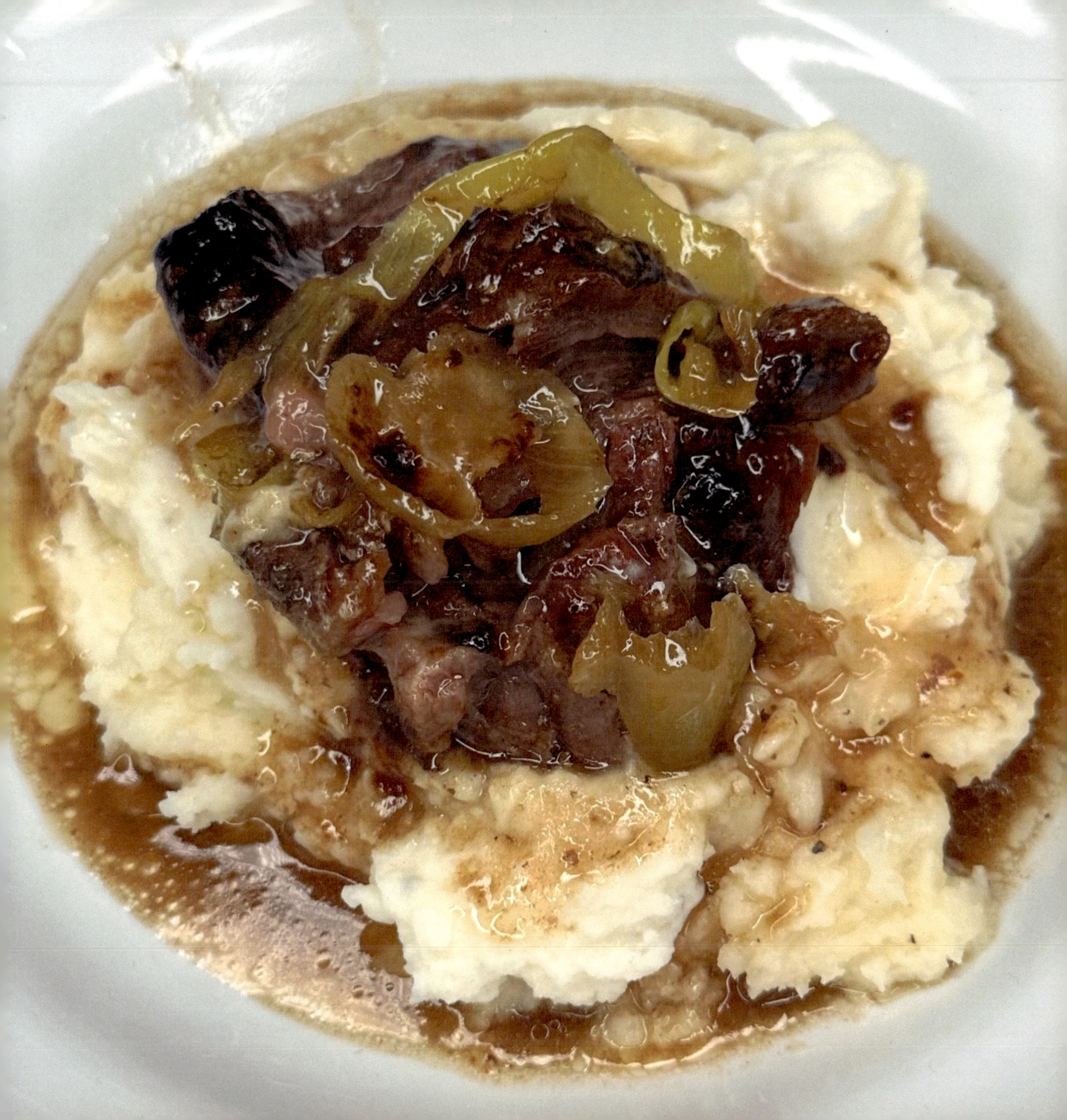

CHILI

SERVES 8-10

INGREDIENTS

Seasoning Blend: 4 tbsp chili powder,

1 tbsp garlic powder,1 tsp cumin, 1 tsp paprika,

1 tbsp parsley flake.

salt, pepper, & crushed red pepper flakes to taste

1-2 tbsp of olive oil

1-2 tbsp of Tabasco

1.5 lbs. of ground beef

2 (28 oz) cans of San Marzano whole peeled tomatoes

2 (16 oz) cans of Dark Red Kidney Beans

1 tbsp of tomato paste

1 chopped onion

1 chopped red bell pepper

10 cloves of chopped garlic

1 bay leaf

1 tsp of cocoa powder (unsweetened)

DIRECTIONS

1. In a dutch oven brown ground beef, fresh garlic, red bell pepper, onion, the seasoning blend, & salt and pepper in olive oil at medium heat.
2. Crush both cans of whole peeled tomatoes with your hands.
3. Add the tomato paste and brown in the pot with the meat mixture.
4. Add the crushed tomatoes and add 1/2 cup of water in the can, swirl it, and add to the pot. Add both cans of beans into the pot including the liquid from the can. Fill one of the bean cans halfway with water, swirl it around and add to the pot.
5. Bring the pot to a rolling boil then lower to a simmer. Then, add Tabasco, a bay leaf, cocoa powder, and crushed red pepper to the pot.
6. Simmer on medium- medium low for about 30-40 minutes. Add water and salt and pepper as needed.
7. Garnish with crushed Fritos, cheddar cheese, chopped green onions, and sour cream.

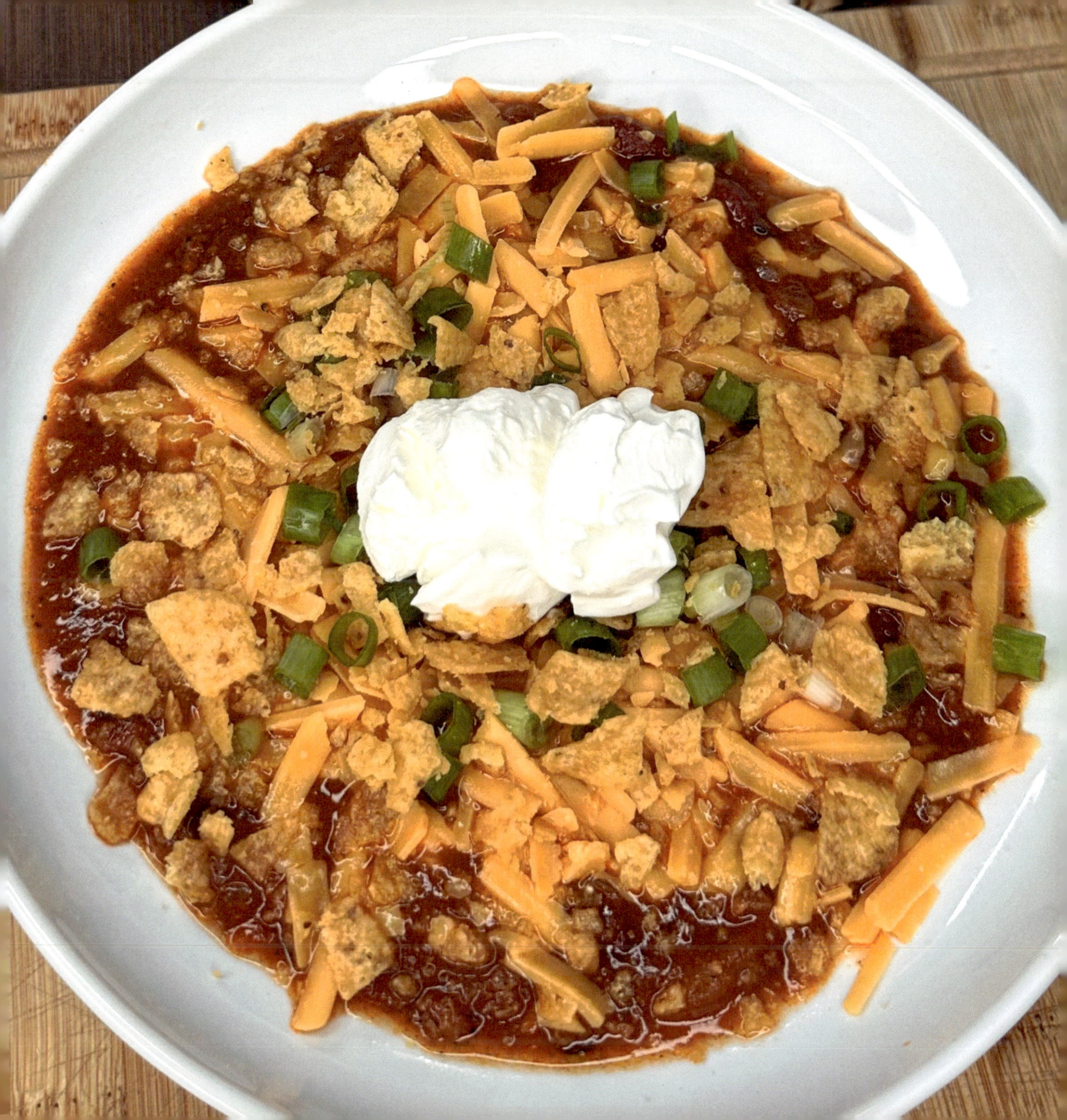

EASY CHEESY ROTINI BAKE

SERVES 6-7

INGREDIENTS

1 tbsp olive oil

1 lb of rotini pasta

1.5 lbs ground beef

1 yellow onion chopped

6 cloves chopped garlic

2 tbsp tomato paste

1 tsp of each: oregano, Italian seasoning blend, garlic powder

2 tsp dried basil

(salt, cracked black pepper and crushed red pepper to taste)

28 oz can of crushed tomatoes

1 cup of pasta water

2 cups whole milk mozzarella

Cheese Balls: 15 oz. ricotta, 1 cup of shredded mozzarella, ½ cup of grated Pecorino or parmesan cheese, ¼ cup of chopped fresh curly parsley, tsp. of salt, tsp of black pepper

DIRECTIONS

1. In a skillet with high sides, brown up ground beef, onions, garlic, seasoning with olive oil.
2. Add a can of crushed tomatoes & about 1/4 cup of water in the can and swirl to get the rest of the tomatoes out into the skillet. Bring to a boil.
3. Boil the rotini until 1-2 minutes before al dente, then add the rotini and 1 cup of pasta water to the skillet. Simmer for about 3-5 minutes.
4. Mix together the ricotta, mozzarella, parsley, grated parmesan, salt, and pepper. Roll into balls.
5. Turn the heat off and add the cheese balls immediately into the skillet. Cover the skillet with 2 cups of whole milk mozzarella.
6. Bake uncovered at 400° F for 20 minutes. Then, broil another minute to brown the cheese.
7. Serve the best dinner ever! Make it!

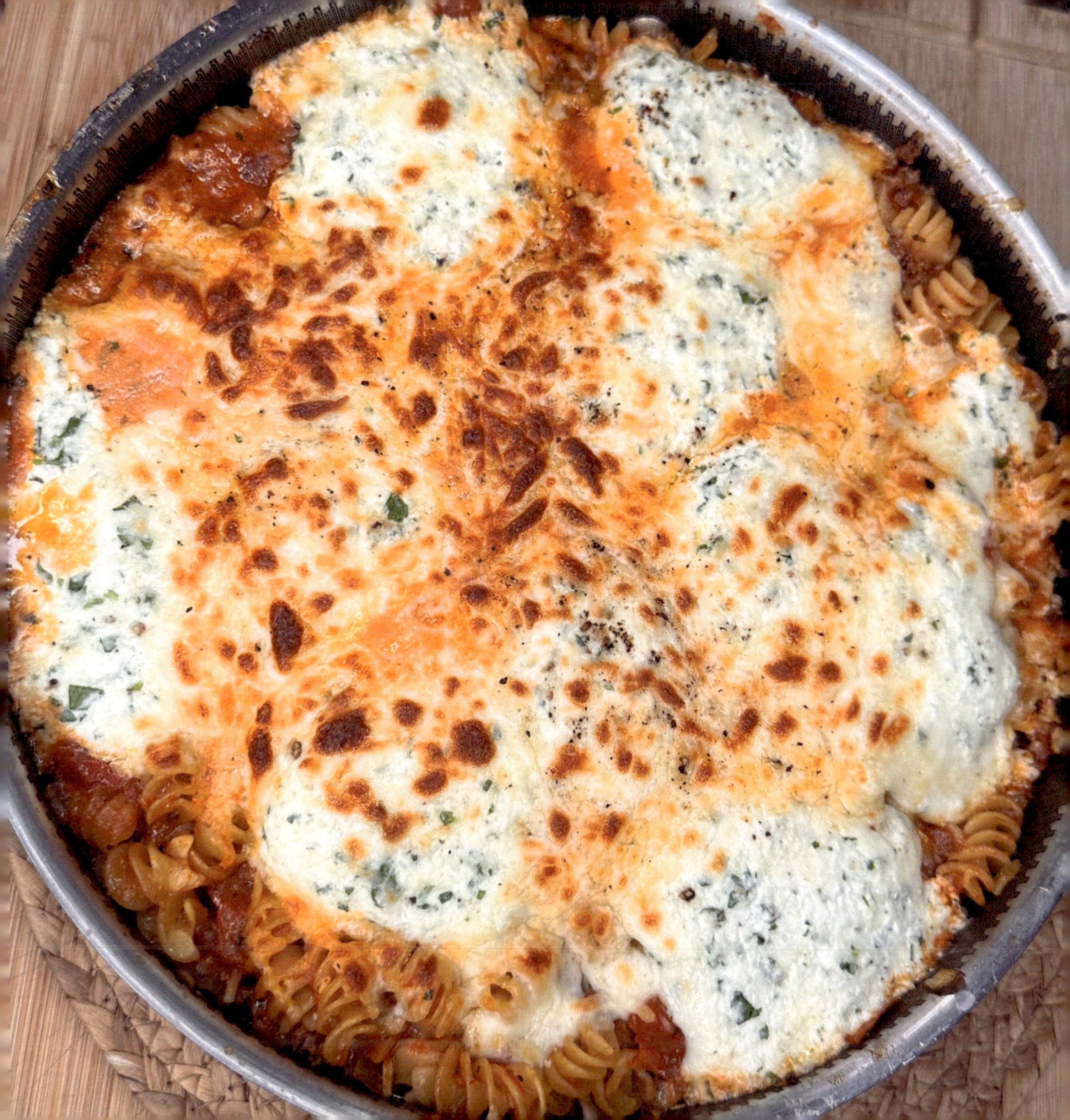

ONE POT BEEF STROGANOFF

SERVES 8

INGREDIENTS

1 tbsp of butter

1 tbsp of olive oil

2.5 cups of egg noodles

16 oz of sliced Baby Bella mushrooms

1 lb ground meat

½ onion chopped

5 cloves of minced garlic

1 tsp salt & pepper (plus more to taste)

2 tbsp of all purpose flour

3-4 oz of white wine

2 ¼ cups beef broth

1 cup of water

½ cup of sour cream plus more for garnish

garnish: chopped green onions

DIRECTIONS

1. In a pan with butter and olive oil, sauté mushrooms at medium heat with salt & pepper until they are soft and golden. Drain any excess liquid from the pan.
2. Add in ground meat, onions, garlic, salt & pepper, and sauté until meat is browned.
3. Shake over the flour and sauté continuously for 2-3 minutes.
4. Deglaze the pan with white wine. Cook for 2 minutes.
5. Add the beef broth and water to the pan and bring the pan to a boil.
6. Once it comes to a boil add in egg noodles (uncooked) directly to the pan stirring them in. Lower pan to medium heat, cover with the lid, and simmer for 5-8 minutes while stirring occasionally.
7. Remove the lid and cook for another 2-3 minutes so the liquid evaporates and the sauce thickens. Turn the heat off and stir in the sour cream.
8. Garnish with sour cream & green onions. ENJOY!!!!

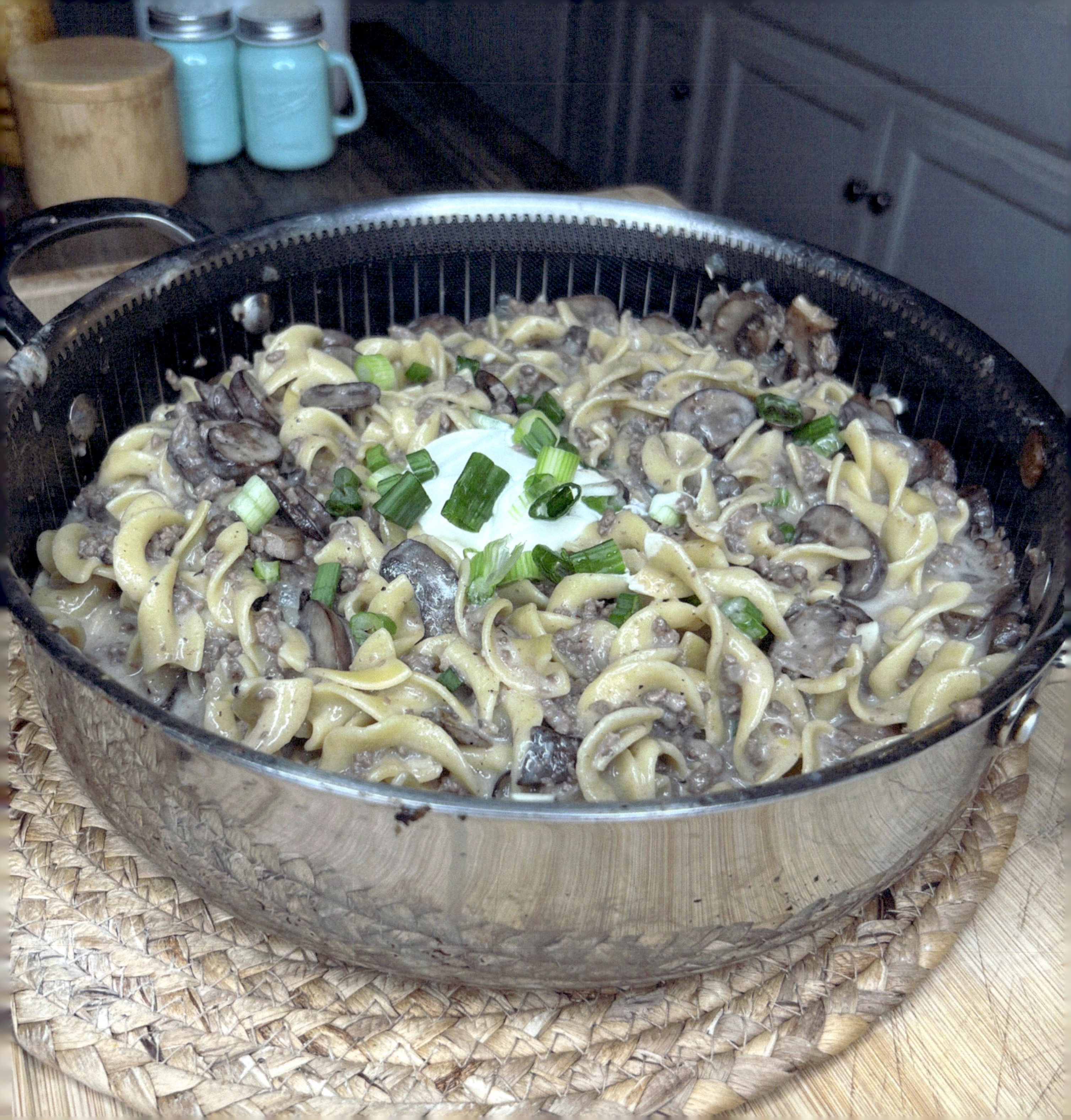

ONE POT UNSTUFFED PEPPERS

SERVES 5

INGREDIENTS

5 hot Italian sausages, casings removed

1 cup of long grain rice

6 cloves garlic, chopped

1 green bell pepper, chopped

1 small onion, chopped

14.5 oz can of diced tomatoes

2 cups of chicken stock

3-4 tbsp of Julienned sun dried tomatoes

½ tsp crushed red pepper

2 tbsp of olive oil

Salt & pepper to taste start with 1 tsp. each and build from there

DIRECTIONS

1. Remove the casings from all 5 sausages. Add them to a pan with 1 tbsp olive oil and separate them with a wooden spoon, potato masher, or your hand.

2. Add in the chopped onion, bell pepper, garlic, sun dried tomatoes, crushed red pepper, 1 tbsp of olive oil, and salt and pepper. Sauté at medium heat until everything is golden and browned. Continue mashing up the sausage with a wooden spoon or masher while it's cooking.

3. Add the rice and sauté for a couple minutes with the rest of the ingredients.

4. Add the entire can of diced tomatoes & chicken stock. Bring the pan up to a rolling boil. Then, immediately once it boils, lower to a low simmer. Cover the pan and cook for about 20-30 minutes or until the rice is cooked and fluffy!

5. Enjoy! SO delicious!!

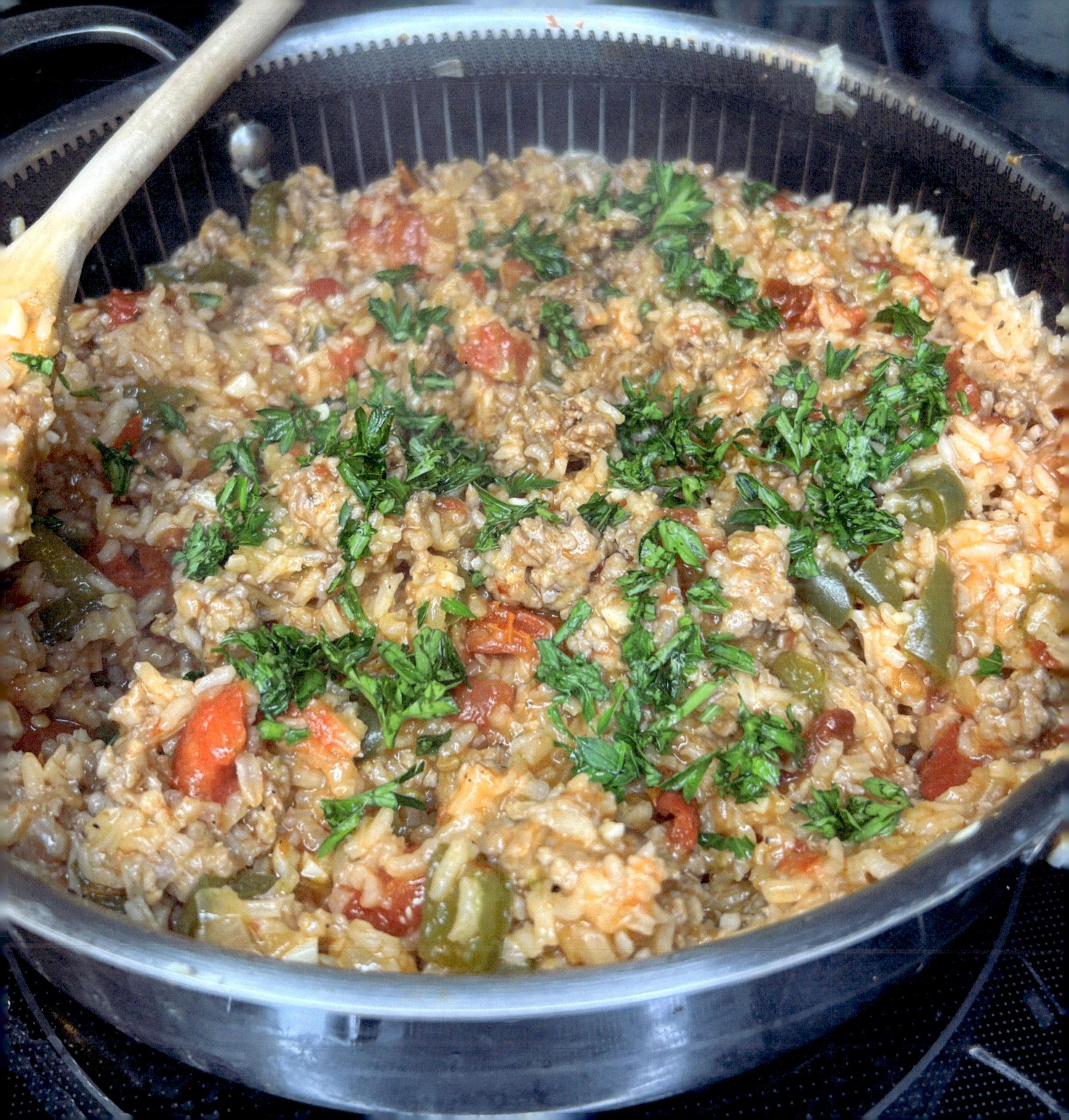

CREAMY SAUSAGE TORTELLINI SOUP

SERVES 6-8

INGREDIENTS

1 lb of hot Italian sausage casings removed

1-2 tbsp of olive oil

1 small onion sliced

6 cloves of chopped garlic

6 oz of sliced white mushrooms

3 tbsp of flour

1 tsp dried basil

½ tsp of oregano

½ tsp of mustard powder

Salt and cracked black pepper to taste

½ tsp of red pepper flakes

1 tsp of hot sauce

¼ tsp of cayenne

2 packages of cheese-stuffed tortellini 18 oz. total

2 oz. hunk of Pecorino Romano Cheese

4 cups of chicken stock

2 cups of heavy cream

8 oz of baby spinach

Fresh parsley and grated Pecorino Romano to taste

DIRECTIONS

1. Start by removing the casings from the hot Italian sausage. In a dutch oven or soup pot, add olive oil and the sausage. Mash it up until it looks like ground beef. Cook over medium heat until browned.

2. Add the sliced onions, chopped garlic, and sliced mushrooms to the pot with the sausage. Season generously with salt and cracked black pepper. Sauté until the vegetables have softened and everything is nicely browned.

3. Sprinkle the flour over the sausSeason the mixture with dried basil, oregano, mustard powder, red pepper flakes, hot sauce, and cayenne.

4. Continue to sauté for an additional 2-3 minutes, ensuring the seasonings are evenly distributed.age and vegetable mixture. Stir constantly for 2-3 minutes, allowing the flour to cook and create a roux.

5. Pour in the chicken broth and bring the mixture to a boil. Once boiling, reduce the heat to a simmer.

6. Add the heavy cream and the hunk of Pecorino Romano cheese. Let the soup simmer uncovered for 5-10 minutes, allowing the cheese to melt and the flavors to meld together.

7. Stir in the fresh baby spinach, and then add the cheese-stuffed tortellini, which should be cooked al dente. As you add the tortellini, allow some of the pasta water to drip into the soup, adding extra flavor.

8. To serve, garnish your creamy sausage and tortellini soup with grated Pecorino Romano cheese and fresh parsley. Enjoy your homemade, comforting bowl of soup!

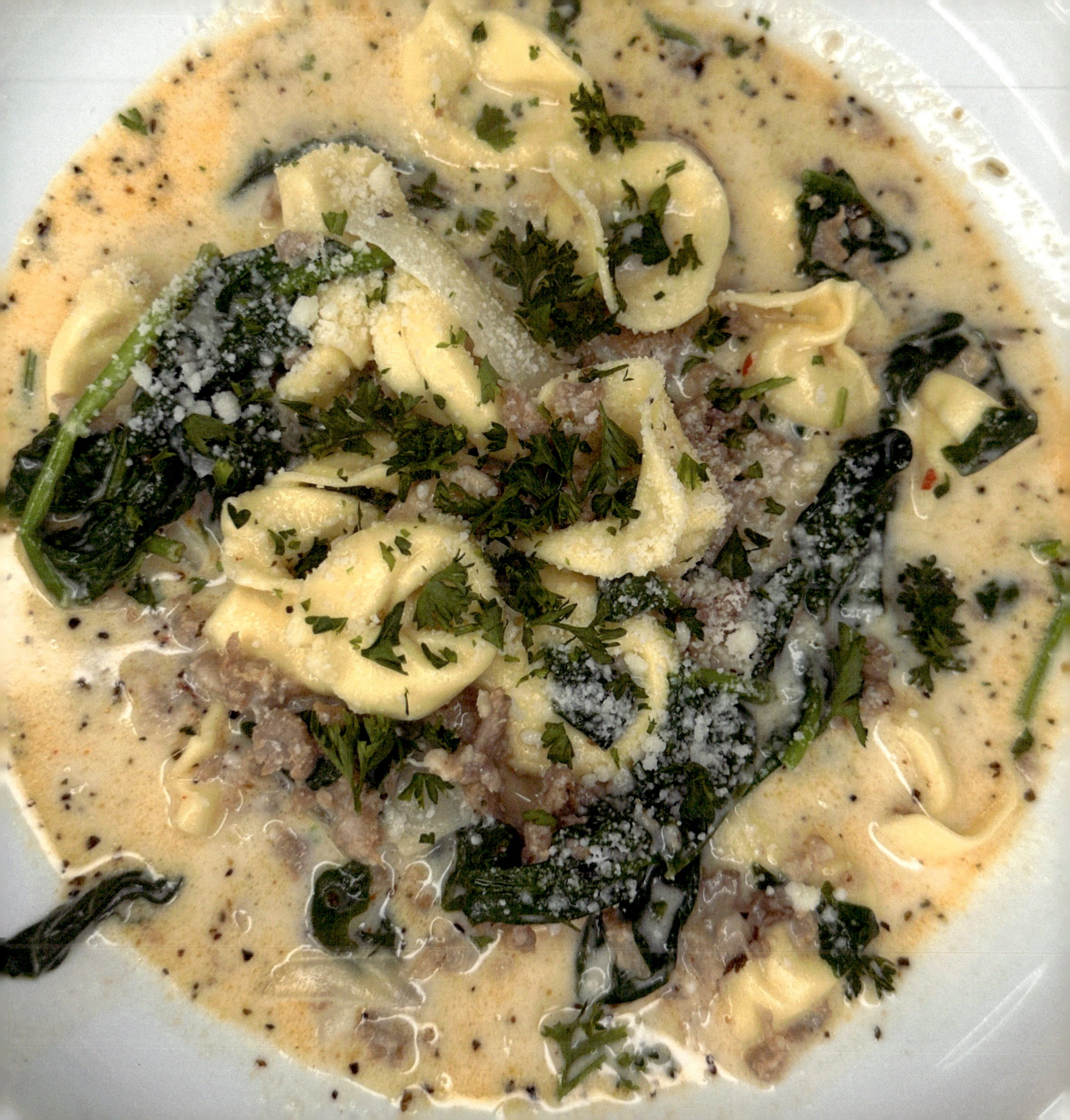

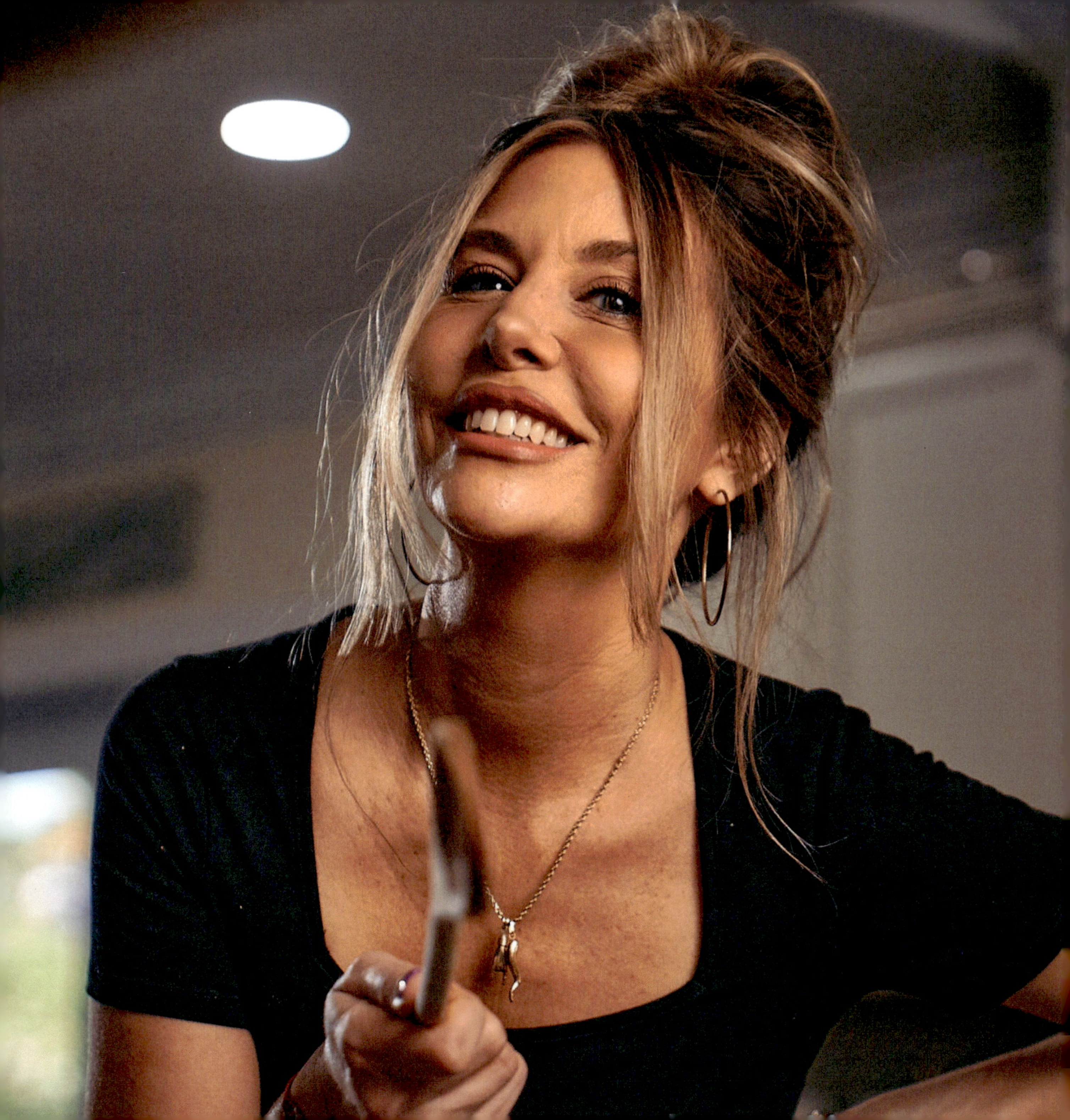

30 Minute Meals

ROASTED TOMATO RICOTTA PASTA

SERVES 6

INGREDIENTS

4-5 cloves of garlic peeled and chopped

7-8 ripe plum tomatoes sliced lengthwise

½ teaspoon of sugar

1 teaspoon of kosher salt

1 teaspoon of cracked black pepper

½ teaspoon of crushed red pepper

2 tablespoons of olive oil

6-8 fresh basil leaves

¼ cup of chopped parsley

16 ounces of ricotta cheese

1 lb pasta of your choice

Pecorino Romano cheese for topping

Fresh chopped parsley and basil for garnish

DIRECTIONS

1. Preheat your oven to 400°F. Grab a sheet pan and line it with aluminum foil for easy cleanup later on.

2. Peel and chop 4-5 cloves of garlic. Spread the garlic evenly over the foil-lined sheet pan. Next, take 7-8 ripe plum tomatoes and slice them lengthwise. Arrange the tomato slices on top of the garlic, making sure to cover the garlic completely. This will prevent it from burning in the oven.

3. Sprinkle sugar, kosher salt, cracked black pepper, & crushed red pepper over the tomatoes. Drizzle olive oil over the tomatoes, making sure they're well coated.

4. Place the sheet pan in the oven and let the tomatoes roast for 15-20 minutes. Keep an eye on them until they become beautifully browned and fragrant.

5. Using the foil as a handy guide, carefully transfer the roasted tomatoes and garlic into a blender. Add fresh basil leaves, fresh parsley, and ricotta cheese to the blender. Blend the mixture until well combined, for about 30 seconds.

6. Cook your pasta according to the until it reaches al dente. Once cooked, drain the pasta and return it to the pot. Pour the delectable roasted tomato and garlic sauce over the pasta and toss it all together until each noodle is coated in the sauce.

7. To add an extra touch of freshness, sprinkle some Pecorino Romano cheese, fresh chopped parsley, and basil over the pasta. Serve it up hot and enjoy the explosion of flavors in every bite!

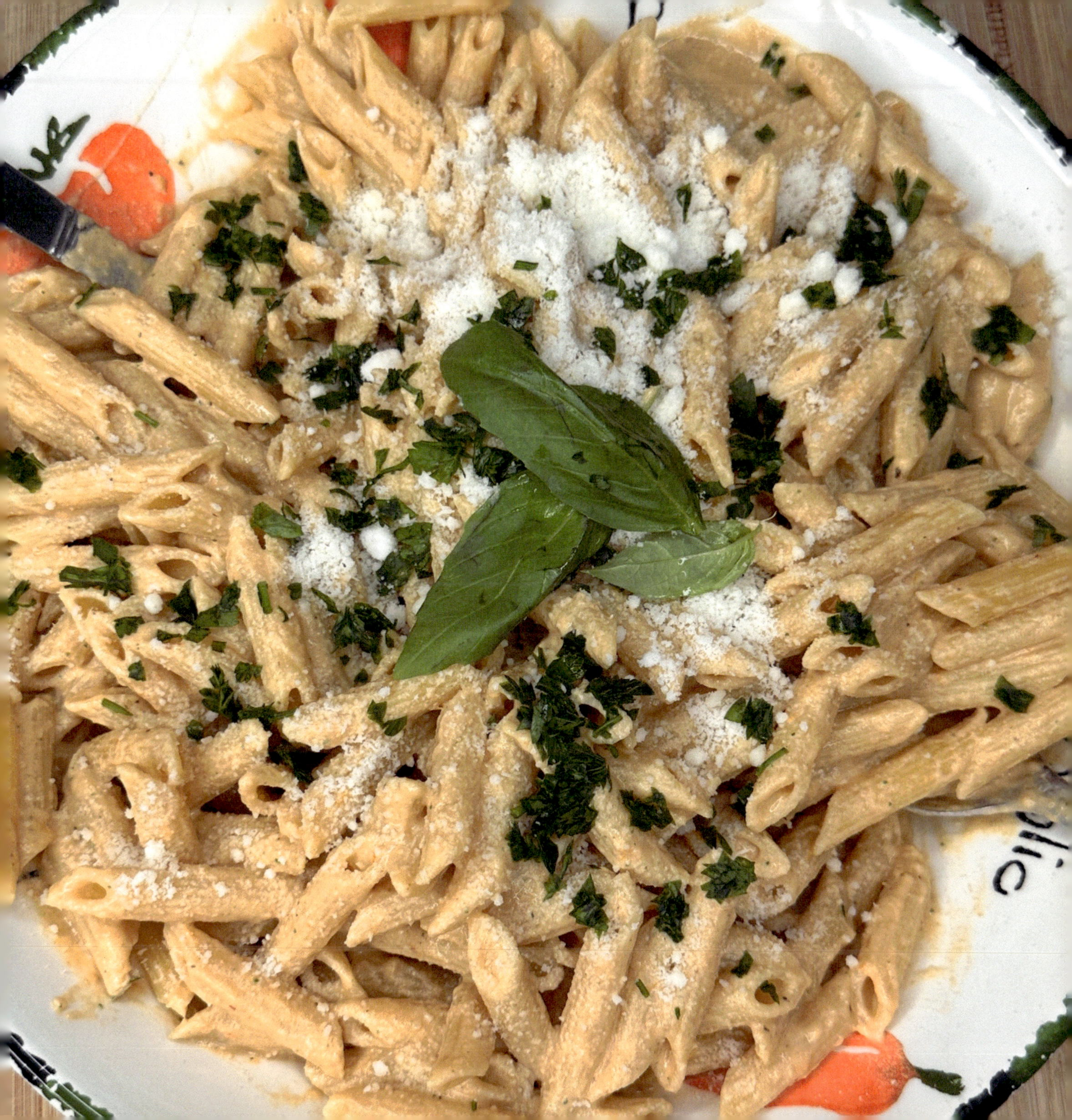

EASY BOURSIN CHICKEN BAKE

SERVES 3-4

INGREDIENTS

1 lb penne pasta cooked until al dente

3 chicken breasts, butterflied

2 packages of original Boursin cheese

1 cup chopped baby spinach

¼ cup chopped parsley, divided

1 tbsp balsamic vinegar

1 tsp brown sugar

2 pints cherry tomatoes

Salt and pepper to taste

1 cup freshly shredded mozzarella cheese

½ red onion, diced

2 tbsp olive oil

DIRECTIONS

1. Preheat your oven to 400°F.

2. In a 9×11 baking dish, add the cherry tomatoes, diced red onions, 1/8 cup of fresh parsley, balsamic vinegar, brown sugar, olive oil, salt, & pepper. Toss the mixture gently to combine all the ingredients. Set it aside.

3. Butterfly the chicken breasts and season with salt & pepper. In a mixing bowl, combine the two packages of Boursin cheese, chopped baby spinach, and 1/8 cup of parsley. Mix the ingredients until well combined.

4. Take the Boursin cheese mixture and press it firmly over each chicken breast, ensuring that the whole chicken breast is covered. Use all of the mixture for all 6 chicken breasts.

5. Place the chicken breasts on top of the tomato mixture in the baking dish. Sprinkle the freshly shredded mozzarella cheese over the chicken breasts. Add cracked black pepper on top for extra flavor.

6. Put the dish in the oven and bake for approximately 30 minutes or until the chicken is nicely browned and the cheese is bubbly and golden.

7. While the chicken is baking, take the cooked penne pasta and toss it with a little butter for added richness.

8. Once the chicken bake is done, remove it from the oven and let it cool for a few minutes. Serve the chicken on a plate alongside the buttered penne pasta. Spoon some of the flavorful tomatoes from the bottom of the pan over the penne pasta. Garnish with fresh parsley for a pop of color.

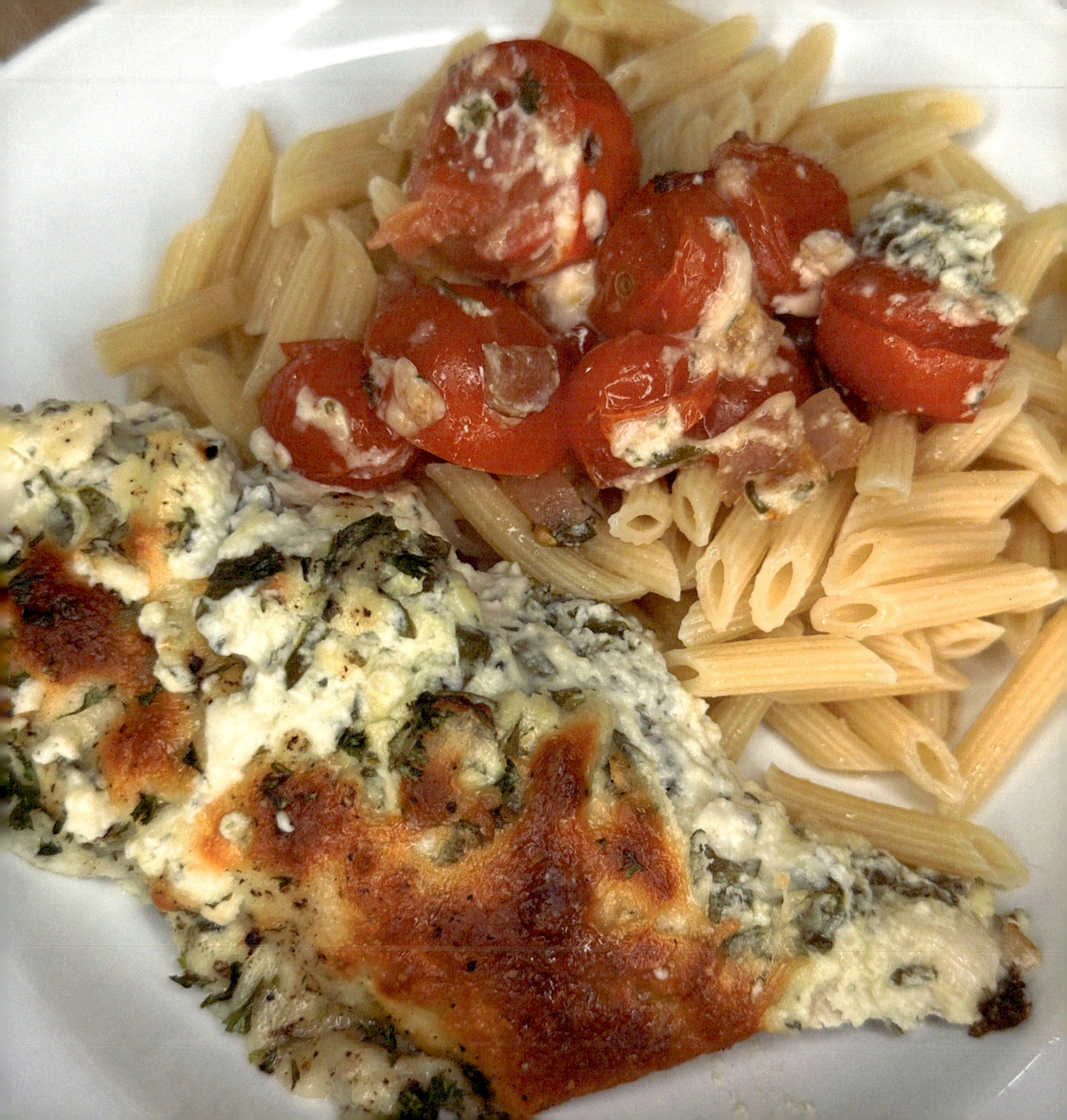

COPYCAT OUTBACK ALICE SPRINGS CHICKEN

SERVES 3-4

INGREDIENTS

¾ cup of mayo

2 tbsp of dijon mustard

¼ cup of honey

3 chicken breasts butterflied

1-2 tsp of garlic salt

Cracked black pepper, to taste

6-7 slices of bacon

8 oz of freshly shredded Colby jack cheese (must be freshly shredded)

8 oz of sliced white mushrooms

1 tbsp of butter

The fat from the bacon

¼ cup of chopped green onions

DIRECTIONS

1. Let's begin by making the dressing. In a bowl, mix together the mayo, dijon mustard, and honey until well combined. Set the dressing aside for later.

2. In a large pan with high sides, fry the bacon until it's crispy. Once done, remove the bacon from the pan and cut each slice in half.

3. Butterfly the chicken breasts and season both sides with garlic salt and cracked black pepper.

4. In the same pan with the remaining bacon grease, sauté the seasoned chicken over medium to medium-high heat until it turns a gorgeous golden brown. This should take about 5 minutes per side. Once cooked, set the chicken aside.

5. Keep the party going in the same pan by adding the sliced white mushrooms. Sauté them in the bacon grease but also add a tablespoon of butter for extra richness. Cook until the mushrooms are golden brown

6. Preheat your oven to 350°F. While the oven is heating up, get a baking sheet and cover it with foil for easy cleanup. Place a rack on top of the baking sheet.

7. It's time to layer the magic! Arrange the chicken on the rack in this order: chicken, a generous portion of the honey mustard dressing you made earlier, sautéed mushrooms, two half slices of bacon on each piece of chicken, and finally, heap on plenty of freshly shredded Colby jack cheese.

8. Pop the baking sheet into the oven and let the chicken bake for around 20 minutes or until the cheese is beautifully melted and golden.

9. Once done, remove the chicken from the oven and get ready to taste the magic! Dunk your Alice Springs Chicken in some extra honey mustard, sprinkle with chopped green onions, and get ready to indulge in your very own Outback adventure at home!

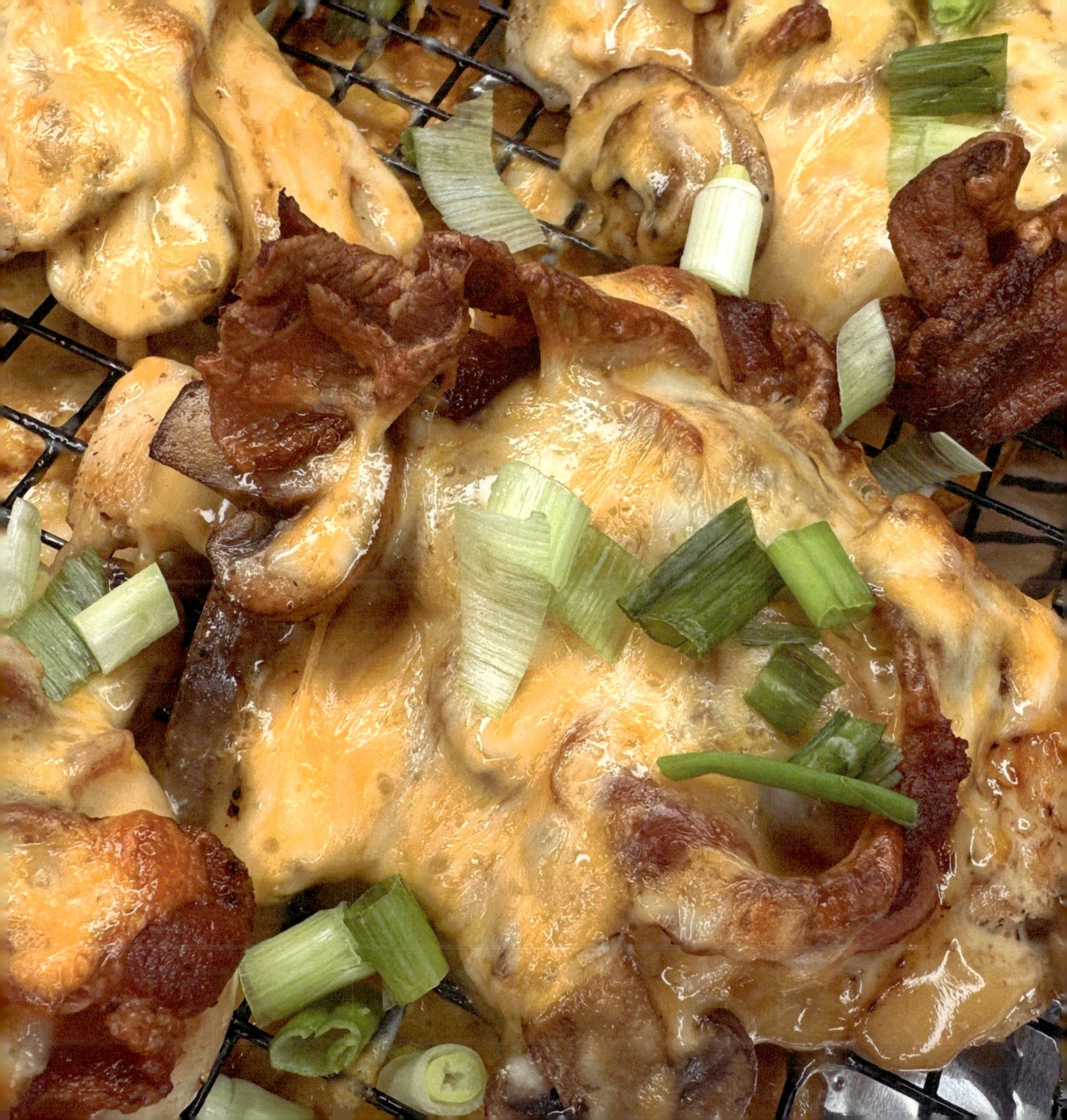

GREEK CHICKEN & TORTELLINI

SERVES 4

INGREDIENTS

Chicken seasoning: 1 tsp smoked paprika 1 tsp oregano, 1 tsp garlic powder, salt, and pepper

4 boneless skinless chicken thighs (patted dry and at room temperature)

Two 10 oz packages of cheese stuffed tortellini

2 tbsp olive oil for sautéing

Salt for pasta water

3-4 oz feta cheese

4 tbsp sliced Kalamata olives

Fresh parsley for garnish

Marinade: 1 cup extra virgin olive oil juice and zest of 1 lemon, 3 tbsp white wine vinegar, 2 tbsp dried minced onions, 5 cloves minced garlic, ¼ cup chopped fresh parsley, 1 tbsp oregano, salt, and pepper

DIRECTIONS

1. Season the chicken with smoked paprika, oregano, garlic powder, and a dash of salt & pepper.

2. It's marinade time! In a bowl, whisk together the olive oil, lemon juice and zest, white wine vinegar, dried minced onions, minced garlic, fresh parsley, oregano, and of course, a pinch of salt and pepper. Set aside about 1/4 cup.

3. Now, take those chicken thighs and let them luxuriate in the rest of the marinade. Cover and pop it into the fridge to marinate for at least 30 minutes – but if you can resist, overnight is even better!

4. Heat up a pan with a touch of olive oil. Lay those marinated chicken thighs into the pan and let them sizzle for about 5-7 minutes on each side.

5. While the chicken is cooking, get your tortellini party started. Boil them up in salted water, then drain. In a separate bowl, toss the cooked tortellini with that reserved marinade you set aside earlier.

6. Slice up your chicken and place it on top of the saucy tortellini. Crumble that feta cheese over the top, Garnish with Kalamata olives & fresh parsley. Your masterpiece is complete!

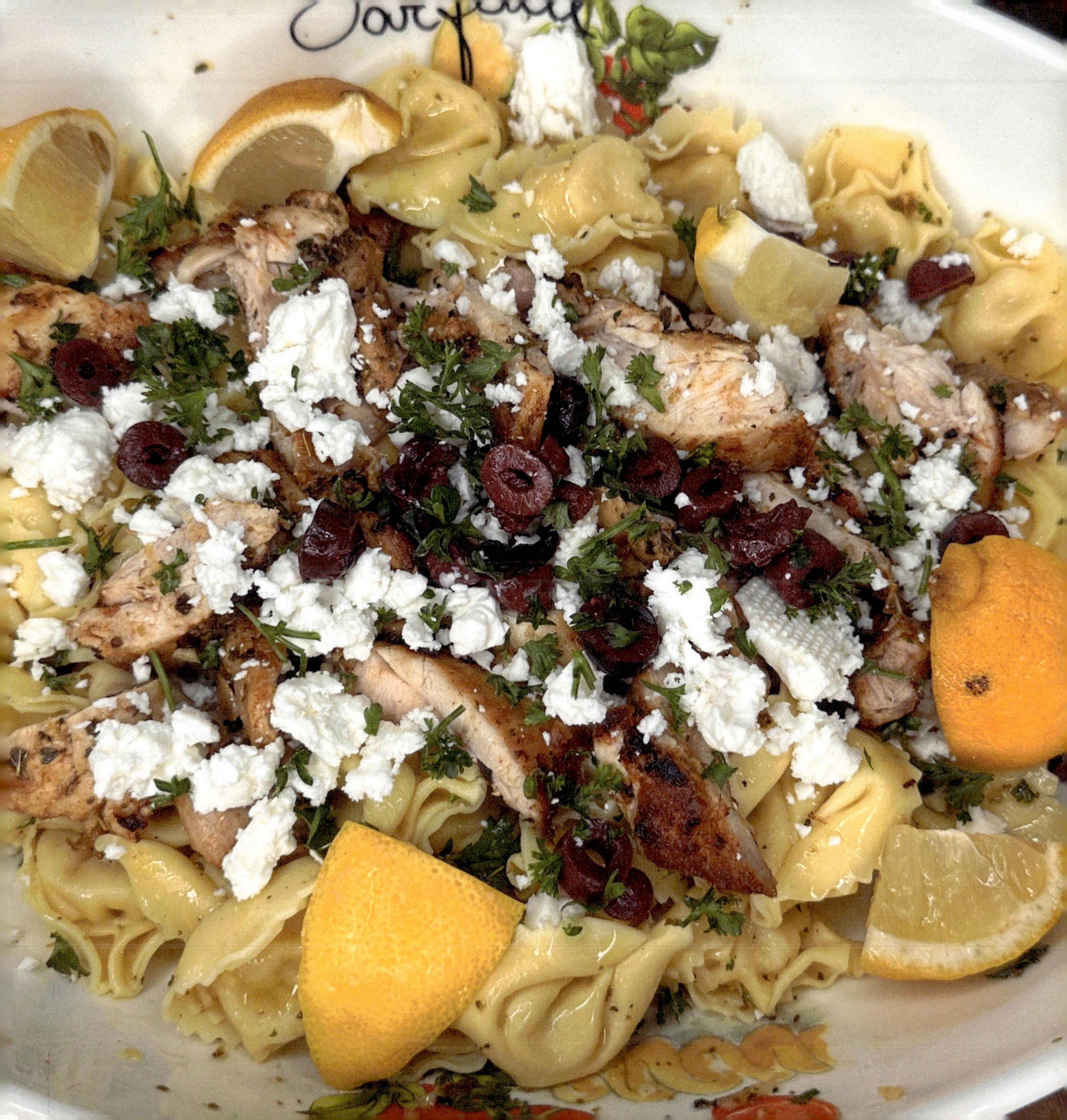

ONE POT CHICKEN & LEMON RICE

SERVES 5-6

INGREDIENTS

4-6 bone-in skin-on chicken thighs

1-2 tbsp. of olive oil

one chopped onion

6-7 cloves of chopped garlic

½ tsp. of crushed red pepper salt & pepper to taste

4 oz. of white wine

1 cup of medium or long grain rice

1.5 cups chicken broth

juice of ½ lemon

zest of ½ a lemon

Chicken seasoning: 1 tsp. garlic powder, 1 tsp. onion powder, 1 tsp. Adobo seasoning, cracked black pepper, 1 tsp. of dried basil, 2 tsp. paprika

1 lemon sliced in rounds

4-5 oz. of julienned sun-dried tomatoes and a tbsp or so of the oil it's packed in

2 tbsp. of tomato paste

¼ cup chopped fresh Italian parsley

DIRECTIONS

1. Season the chicken thighs with the chicken seasoning blend mentioned in the ingredients section. Marinate the chicken thighs for 30 minutes.

2. Pat the chicken things dry after marinating and brown in a skillet with high sides with olive oil. Brown the chicken for about 5 minutes each side. The chicken will cook all the way through in the oven so only cook until browned and glazed. Remove from the pan and set aside on a plate.

3. In the same skillet at medium/high heat add more olive oil if needed and sauté the lemon rounds, onions, chopped garlic, sun dried tomatoes, tomato paste, lemon zest, crushed red pepper, salt, and pepper until golden.

4. Deglaze the skillet with white wine. Allow the alcohol to burn out for a couple minutes in the pan. Then, add the juice of 1/2 a lemon.

5. Add the rice and sauté for a minute or so. Then add the chicken stock. Bring the contents of the skillet to a boil. Then, lower the heat to medium and add the chicken thighs and all of the juices back into the pan

6. Cover the skillet with the lid and cook in the oven 400 degrees°F for 40 minutes.

7. Remove from the oven and garnish the dish with chopped fresh parsley! Enjoy!

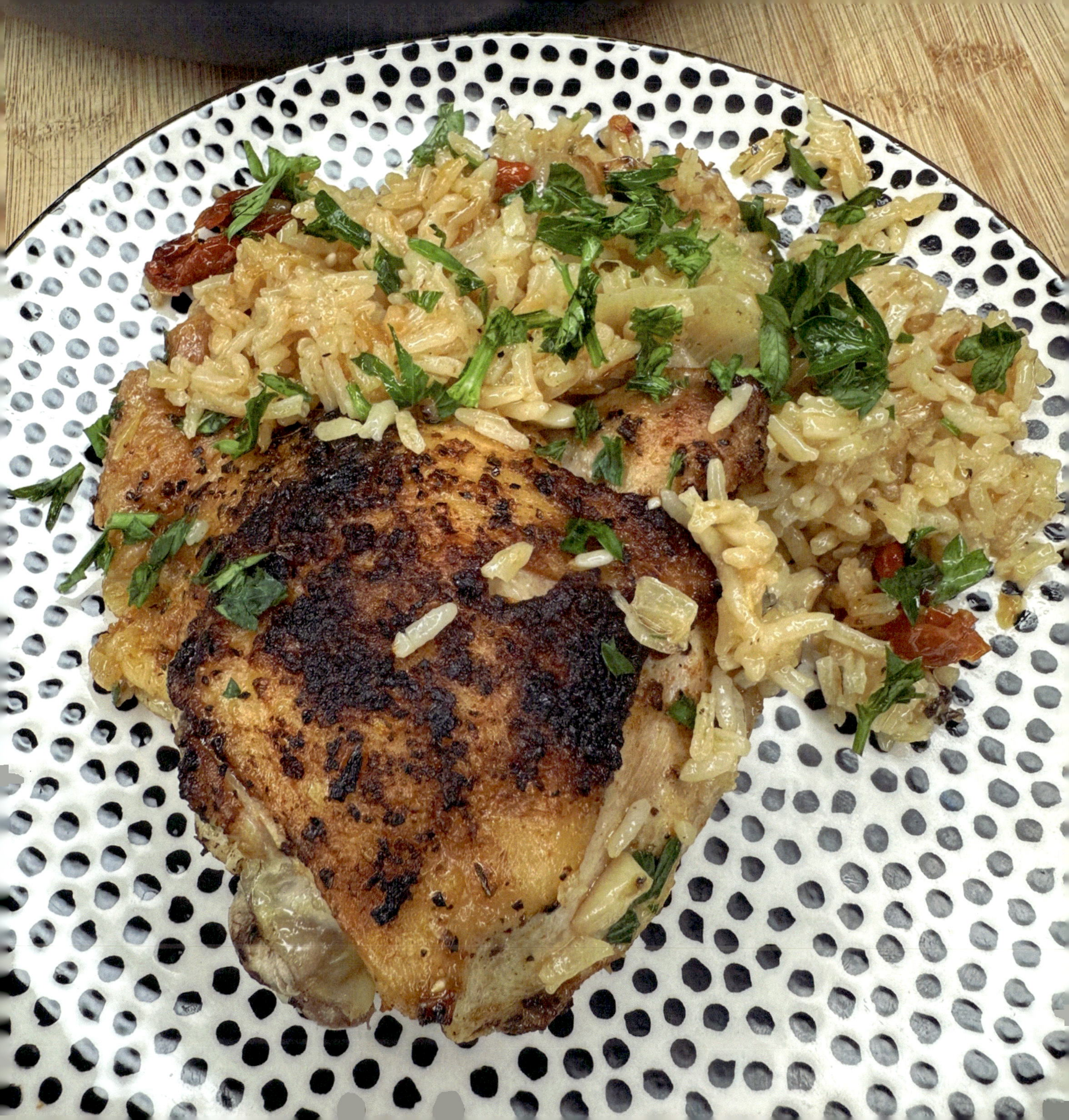

JIFFY JOES

SERVES 6-8

INGREDIENTS

1-2 lbs of ground chuck

15 oz can of Manwich Original

15 oz can of Manwich Bold

2 boxes of Jiffy Mix (8.5 oz boxes)

2 eggs

1 cup of milk

2 cups of shredded cheddar jack cheese

1 small onion chopped

6-7 cloves of garlic chopped

¼ cup of shredded cheddar (for topping)

Seasoning: 1 tsp of garlic powder, 1 tsp of smoked paprika, ¼ tsp of cayenne pepper, salt and pepper to taste

DIRECTIONS

1. Seasoning: 1 tsp of garlic powder, 1 tsp of smoked paprika, 1/4 tsp of cayenne pepper, salt and pepper to taste

2. While that's browning, mix together in a bowl: two boxes of Jiffy mix, milk, & eggs. Blend with an electric mixer just until incorporated. Then, fold in 2 cups of cheddar cheese. Set aside.

3. Once the meat is browned, add both cans of Manwich and mix together. Bring to a boil, then lower to a simmer. Simmer on medium low until the flavors are incorporated (about 5 minutes or so). Taste for seasoning and add more if needed.

4. With an ice cream scoop , scoop all of the Jiffy mixture on top of the meat mixture. Make it even if you desire by spreading it with a knife. Top with cheddar cheese and bake at 350° F for 35-40 minutes. Let it rest for 10 minutes and serve! Delicious!

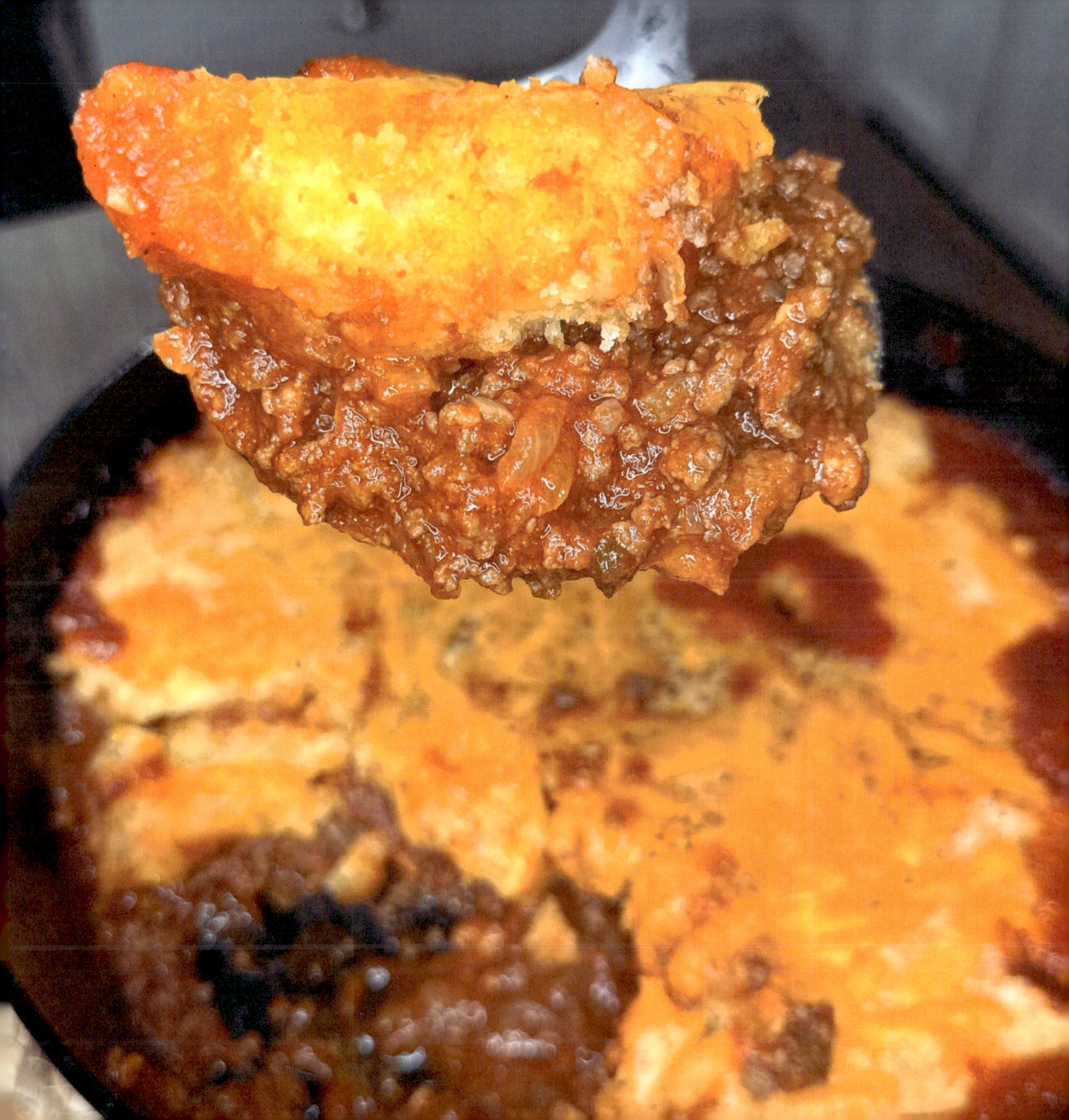

CHICKEN PICCATA

SERVES 3-4

INGREDIENTS

3 chicken breasts, butterflied and pounded thin

2 cups of flour

2 lemons

8 oz of white wine Chardonnay or Pinot Grigio

1.5 cups of chicken broth

2 tbsp of flour mixed + 2 tbsp of softened butter, to make a paste

¼ cup of chopped fresh parsley

¼ cup of capers

1-2 tsp of salt for the flour and chicken

1-2 tsp of cracked black pepper for the flour and chicken

More salt & cracked black pepper to taste for the sauce

DIRECTIONS

1. Butterfly chicken breasts and then pound them nice and thin. Add salt & pepper to each side and make sure it's patted dry.
2. Add all purpose flour to a bowl and generously add salt and pepper to the flour. Dredge the cutlets into the flour and set aside
3. In a pan with butter & olive oil sauté the chicken on each side for 5-10 minutes. Set the chicken aside.
4. Then discard a little bit of the oil if it's very full (leave about 2 tbsp of oil) but do NOT clean out the pan. You need the flavors of the chicken in the pan.
5. Make a flour paste: mix together 2 tbsp of flour with 2 tbsp of softened butter (or water works too)
6. To the pan add 1 lemon sliced in rounds & sauté each side. Then deglaze the pan with about 1 cup of white wine (bring to low boil to burn alcohol out).
7. Add about 1 & 1/2 cups of chicken broth and the juice of 1/2 a lemon.
8. Add flour paste and whisk continuously for 3-5 minutes. Add salt & pepper to taste! Add chopped fresh parsley and 3-4 tbsp of caper.
9. Simmer for about 5-10 minutes then add chicken back to the pan.
10. Simmer together for about 10 minutes. Serve over mashed potatoes or rice!

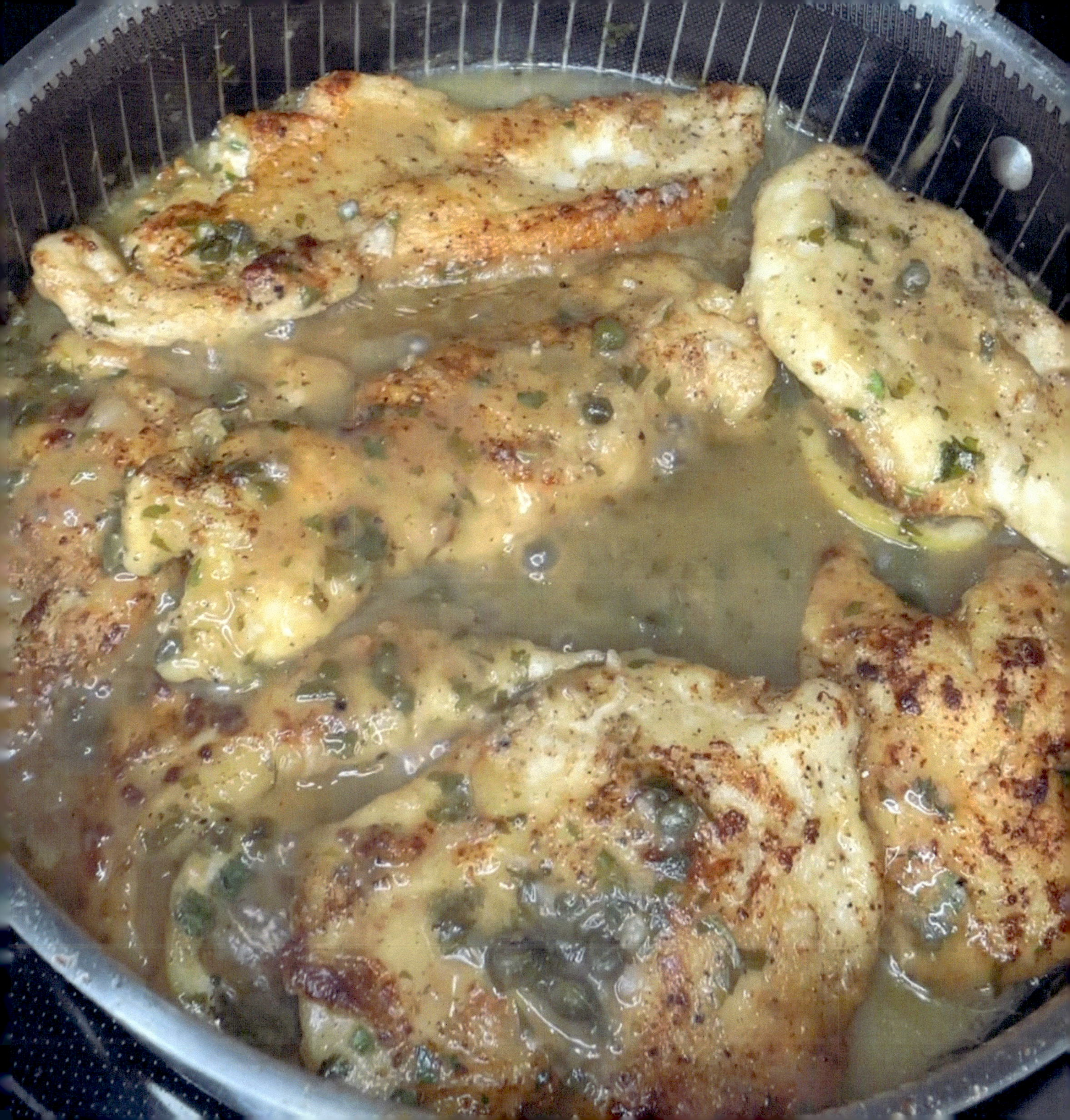

EASY BEEFARONI

SERVES 6

INGREDIENTS

1.5 lbs ground beef (I use ground chuck)

1 yellow onion diced

5-7 cloves of garlic minced

1-2 tbsp of Italian seasoning blend

Cracked black pepper and salt to taste

½ tsp of crushed red pepper

1 can of all purpose crushed tomatoes 28 oz.

About 1 cup of pasta water

A handful of fresh basil

About ¼ cup of Pecorino Romano grated Cheese

1 lb. of Rigatoni (I use number 27 size)

DIRECTIONS

1. Add ground beef, chopped onion, minced garlic, Italian seasoning, crushed red pepper, and salt & pepper to a skillet with high sides. Cook on medium heat until the meat is almost cooked through and the onions and translucent.

2. In the meantime, boil the rigatoni according to the directions on the back of the box to achieve al dente pasta.

3. Add the can of crushed tomatoes to the sauce once the ground beef is almost cooked all the way through.

4. Bring the contents of the pan to a boil; then lower to a medium low heat and simmer on the stove until the pasta is nearly finished cooking.

5. Add a ladle full of pasta water (about 1 cup) to the sauce once the pasta is nearly finished cooking and let the sauce simmer until creamy. (about 3-5 minutes)

6. Once you achieve the desired consistency add fresh basil and Pecorino Romano to the sauce and mix and simmer for another couple minutes.

7. Add the pasta directly to the pan and simmer together.

8. Serve it all up and enjoy!

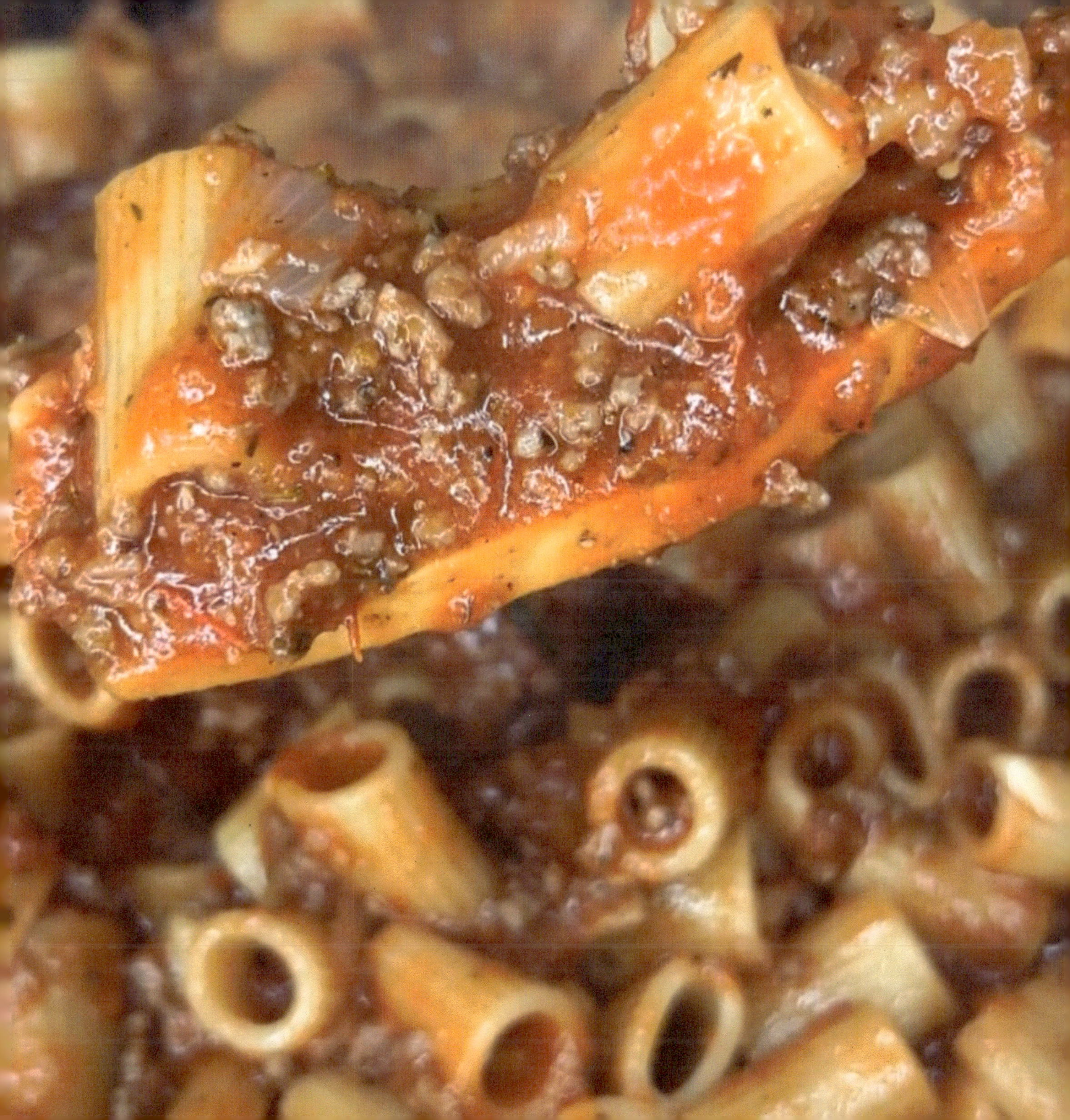

CRAB STUFFED SALMON

SERVES 3

INGREDIENTS

2-3 servings of salmon

6 oz. can of lump crab meat, drained

4 oz. softened cream cheese

¼ cup grated pecorino romano cheese

14 Ritz crackers, crushed

Juice of 1 lemon, divided

Zest of ½ lemon

1 tsp Tony's Creole seasoning

1/2 packet of Sazon seasoning

½ packet of Sazon seasoning

4 tbsp of melted butter

¼ cup of each: chopped green onions & fresh parsley, divided

2 tsp of paprika, divided

½ tsp of each: garlic & onion powder

About 1 tbsp of cracked black pepper, divided

DIRECTIONS

1. Score each piece of salmon lengthwise across the top of the salmon filets. (don't cut through...just make a little slit to hold the stuffing. Season with 1 tsp of paprika, garlic and onion powder and black pepper.

2. Combine the cream cheese, lump crab meat, chopped garlic, pecorino cheese, crushed Ritz crackers, juice & zest of 1/2 lemon, Creole and Sazon seasoning, 1 tsp of paprika, black pepper & the majority of the chopped fresh parsley and green onions. Gently fold and mix until combined to keep the crab intact.

3. Stuff the salmon generously with the stuffing & Place in a baking dish.

4. Melt 4 tbsp of butter & whisk in the rest of the green onions & parsley and the juice of 1/2 a lemon and cracked black pepper. Pour over stuffed salmon. Bake at 350° F for about 20-25 minutes. Serve over mashed potatoes! Enjoy!

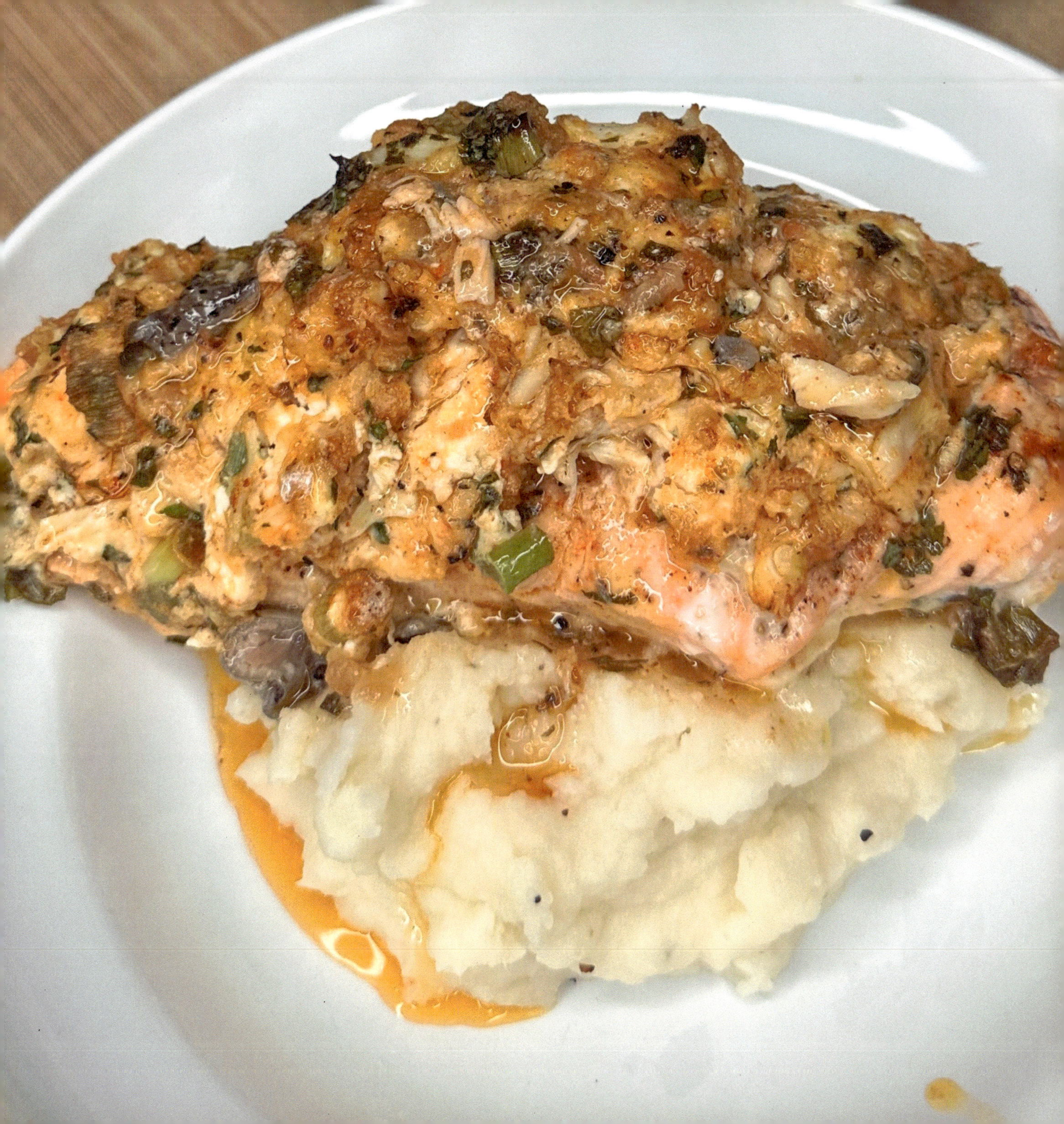

ONE POT CREAMY STEAK PASTA

SERVES 5-6

INGREDIENTS

1 lb fusilli pasta

2 New York strip steaks

6 garlic cloves, chopped

1 shallot, sliced

½ stick butter + 1 tbsp butter, divided

2 tbsp olive oil

1 & ½ cups heavy cream

½ cup chicken stock

6 oz sliced white mushrooms

2 handfuls of baby spinach

¼ cup chopped fresh parsley

1 cup pasta water

½ cup grated pecorino romano

1 tbsp tomato paste

2 tsp Montreal seasoning & 1 tsp Italian herb seasoning

1 tbsp flour

1 tsp garlic powder, onion powder, & paprika

DIRECTIONS

1. Season your steaks on both sides with Italian herb and Montreal seasoning.

2. In a pan sear both the steaks on the fat cap side first, then sear on each side for 5 minutes. While the steak is searing add in 1/2 a stick of butter and baste the steak with the butter while it's cooking.

3. Bring a pot of water to bowl, salt your water, add in the pasta, and cook until al dente.

4. Once steak is seared on both sides, add in shallots, garlic, mushrooms, olive oil, and sauté until mushrooms are golden brown. Then add in tomato paste and brown it for about 3 minutes.

5. Deglaze pan with chicken stock. Add spinach, garlic powder, onion powder, paprika, and saute together for a few minutes. Then add in the heavy cream and pasta water.

6. To make the flour paste to thicken the sauce, add equal parts flour and butter (1 tbsp of each) to a bowl and mash it together, once it becomes a paste add it to your sauce and whisk it continuously for 2-3 minutes. Then add in grated Pecorino Romano, lower the heat, and whisk it together.

7. Stir the cooked pasta into the sauce and top with fresh parsley. Pour the steak juices into the pasta. Slice the steak and place it on top of the pasta. Enjoy!

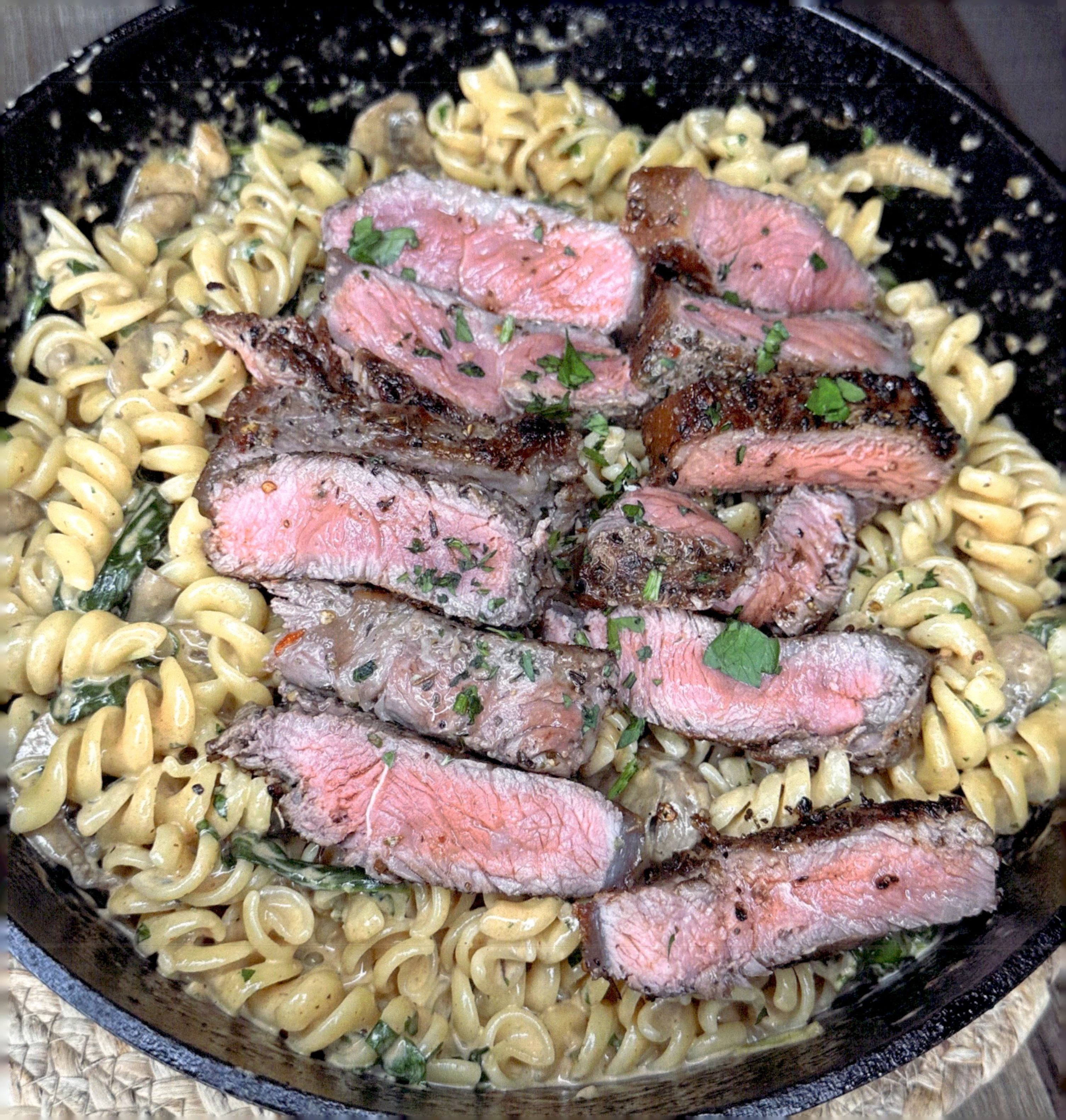

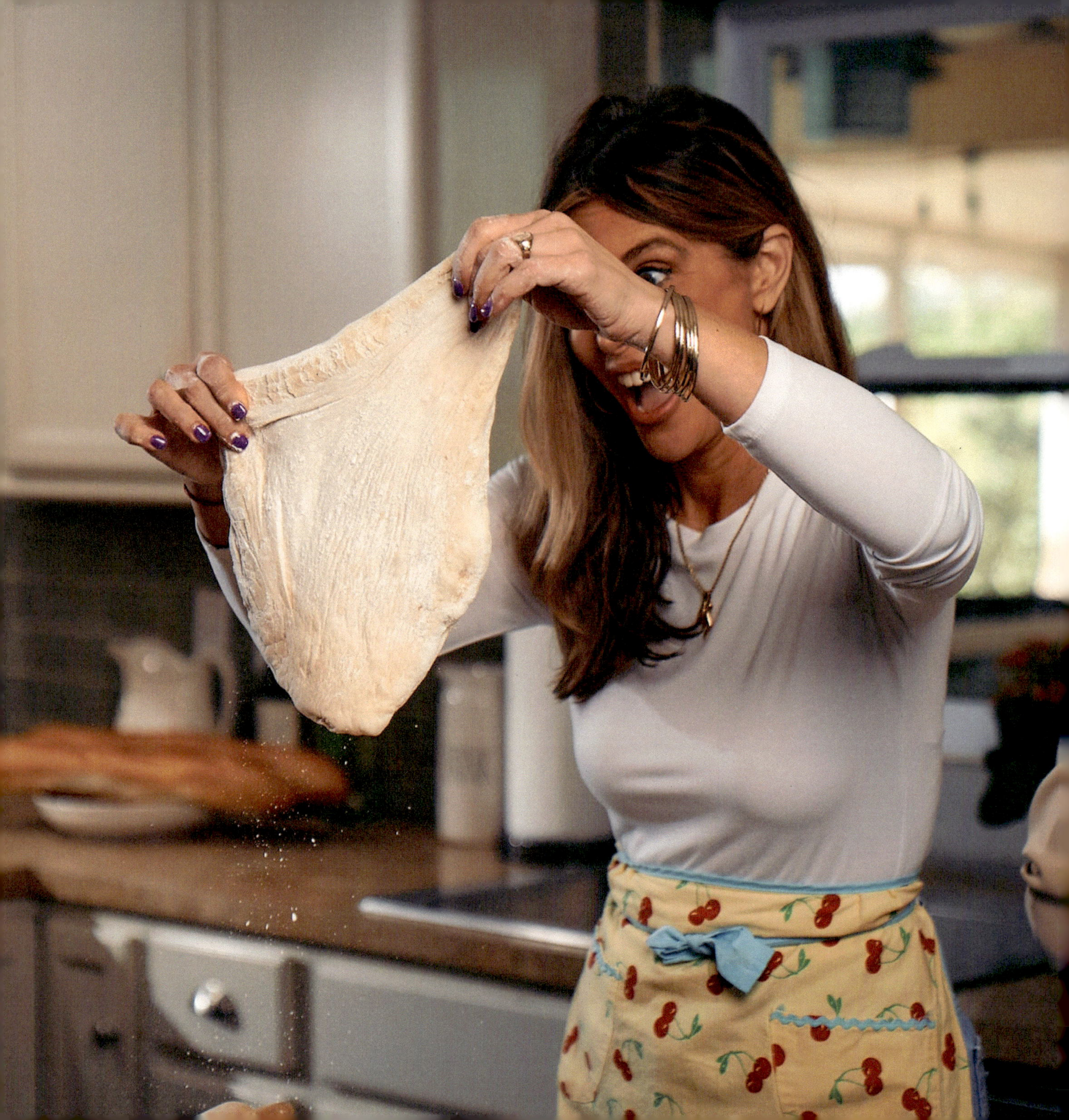

Party Pleasers

CROCKPOT SPINACH ARTICHOKE DIP

SERVES 8-10

INGREDIENTS

1 cup mayo

1 cup sour cream

8 oz of cream cheese

8 oz of frozen spinach

14 oz can Vigo quartered artichoke hearts

1 cup marinated artichokes

2 cups shredded whole milk mozzarella

½ cup grated Pecorino Romano

5 garlic cloves, chopped

2 tbsp dried minced onion

1 tbsp garlic cheese seasoning

½ tsp crushed red pepper flakes

1 tsp salt & pepper

DIRECTIONS

1. In a crockpot add in frozen spinach, mayo, sour cream, cream cheese, can of drained & chopped artichoke hearts, and marinated artichoke hearts (you don't need to drain these, about 1 tbsp of the marinated juice will go in with the artichokes.)

2. Next add in shredded mozzarella cheese, grated Pecorino Romano, chopped garlic, dried minced onion, garlic cheese seasoning, crushed red pepper flakes, and salt & pepper.

3. Put the top on the crockpot and cook on high for 2 - 3 hours.

4. After 2 hours stir the dip to see how much longer it has.

5. serve with bread or chips. Enjoy!!! Make it!!!!

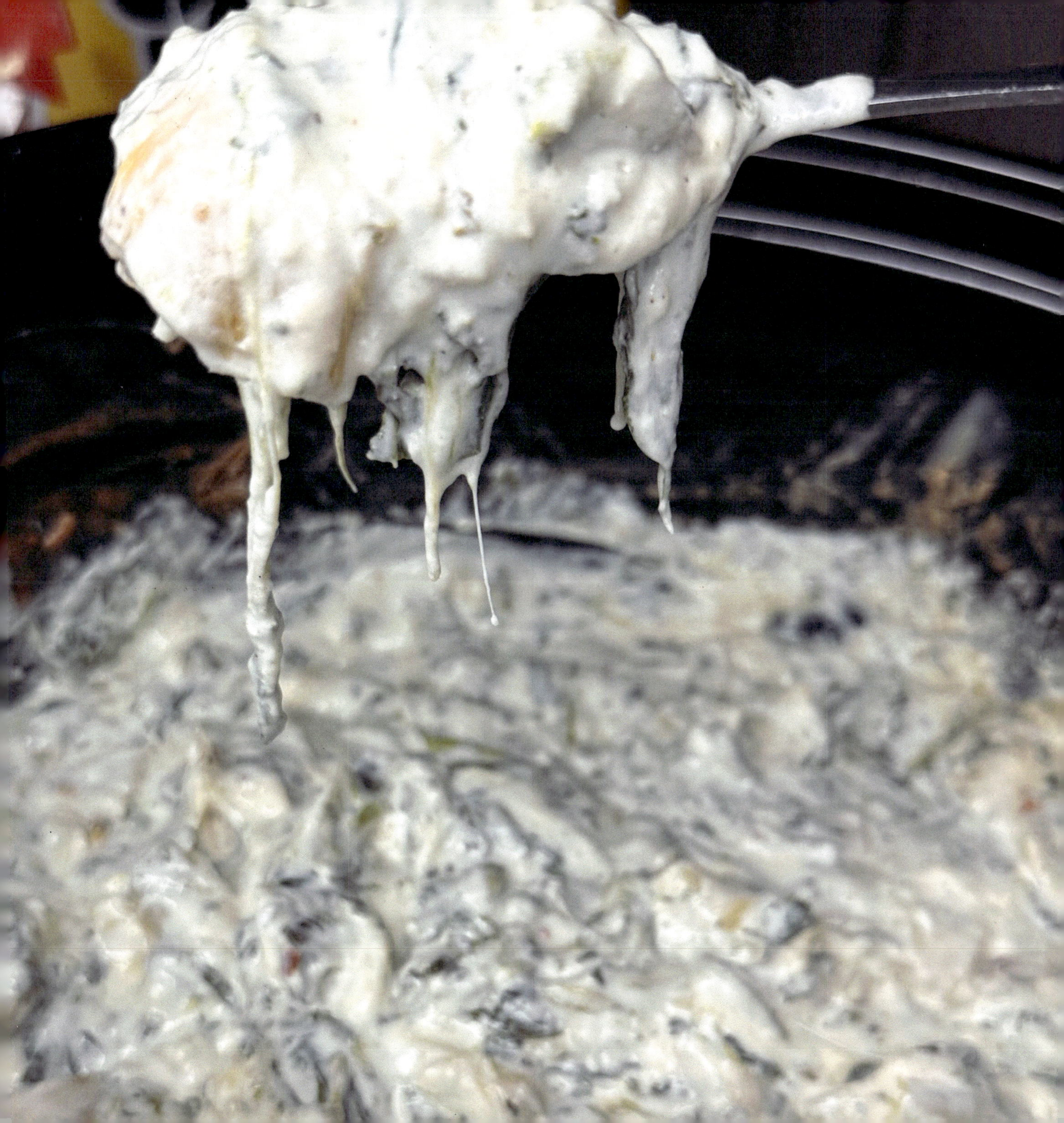

EASY ONION DIP

SERVES 8-10

INGREDIENTS

2 large diced sweet onions

2 cups of mayonnaise

16 oz of freshly shredded Swiss cheese

¼ cup of shredded mozzarella

salt and cracked black pepper to taste

1 large bread bowl (I used cranberry walnut bread bowl from Costco)

DIRECTIONS

1. Grate the Swiss cheese.
2. Mix together the diced onions, shredded Swiss cheese, and mayonnaise. Add salt and lots of cracked black pepper to taste.
3. Add into a baking dish (I used a 9 x 13).
4. Bake at 350° F for about 45 minutes or until browned and bubbly.
5. Hollow out the bread bowl and add the baked onion dip into the bread bowl. Chop up the extra bread you removed into cubes and use for dipping.
6. Place the filled bread bowl on a baking sheet lined with foil or parchment paper and top the onion dip with mozzarella and more cracked black pepper.
7. Set the oven to broil and cook until the top is browned... about 2-3 minutes. Serve and enjoy!

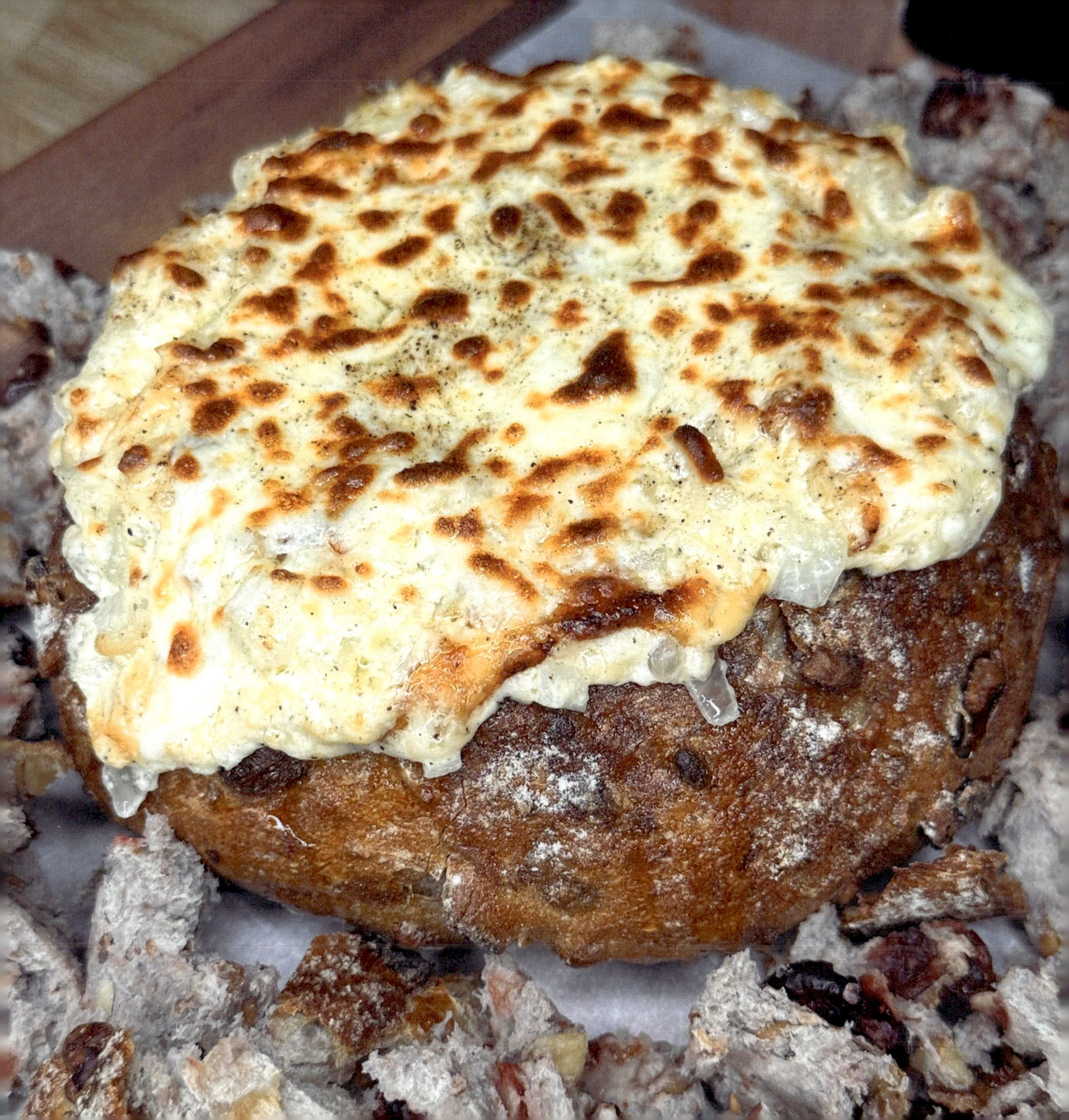

ROAST BEEF & AJU SLIDERS

SERVES 6-8

INGREDIENTS

¼ lb Boar's head cheddar cheese, sliced thin

½ lb Boar's head roast beef, rare & sliced thin

¼ lb muenster cheese, sliced thin

¾ stick butter, melted

1 tbsp from an Au Jus Gravy packet

Couple shakes of worcestershire

1 pack king's hawaiian rolls

½ tsp onion powder

1 tsp dried minced onion

Salt & pepper, to taste

Sesame seeds

DIRECTIONS

1. Slice open sweet rolls and add the bottom half to a greased 9 x 13 baking sheet.
2. Layer 1: Boar's head cheddar cheese
3. Layer 2: Boar's head roast beef
4. Layer 3: Muenster cheese
5. In a bowl mix: melted butter, au jus powder from a packet, worcestershire, sesame seeds, & dried minced onions & onion powder & salt & pepper!
6. Top your sliders & pour over the butter sauce.
7. Bake at 350°F covered with foil for 15 minutes and uncovered for another 15 minutes.
8. Dipping sauce: fill the bowl you used to make the butter sauce with 2 cups of water, add to a saucepan, bring to a boil, add the rest of the au jus gravy packet, then lower to a simmer until you notice the au jus getting a little thicker!
9. Remove your sliders, slice them up, dip, dip dippity do and enjoy the best sliders ever.

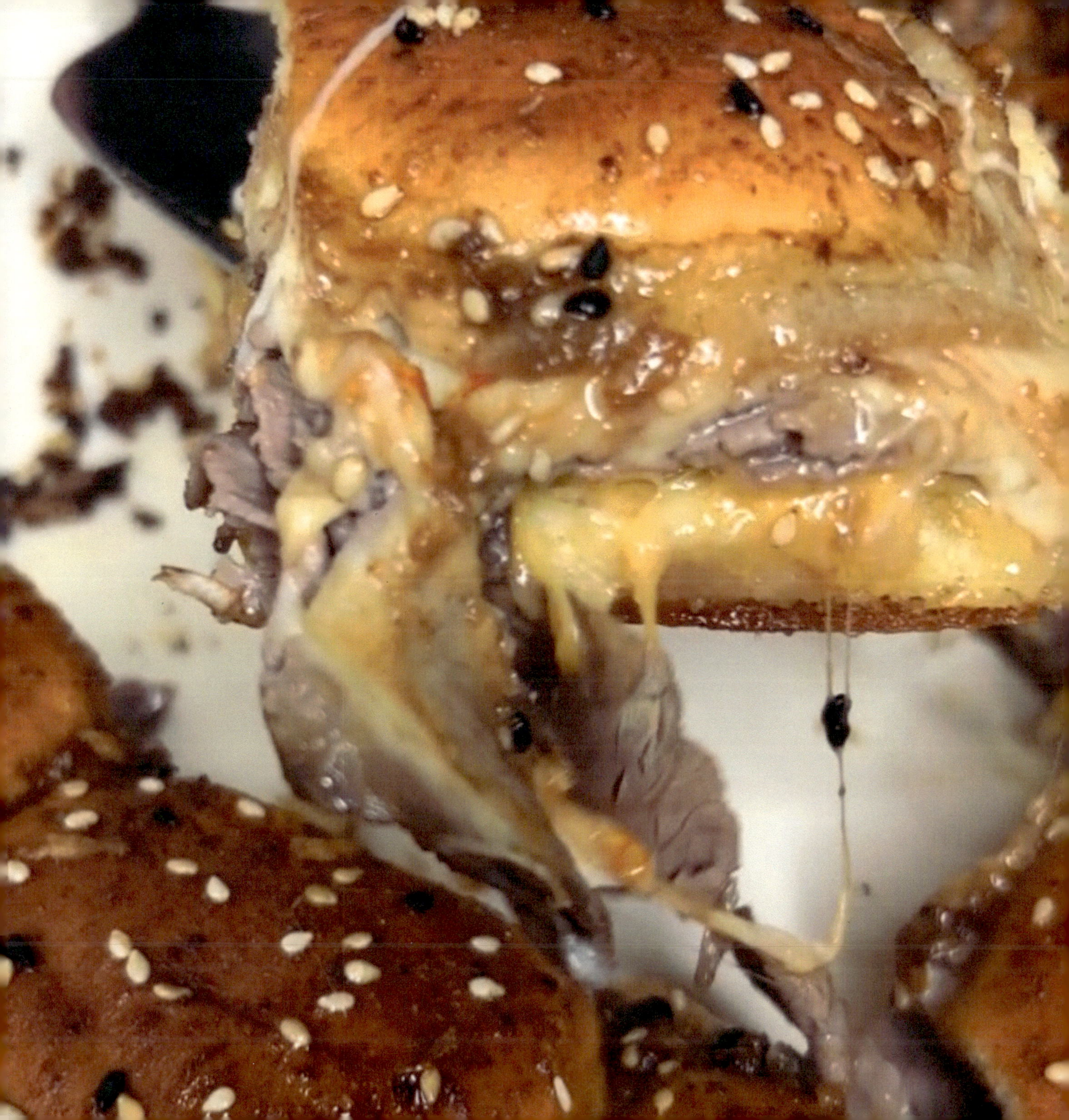

BIG MAC SLIDERS

SERVES 6-8

INGREDIENTS

2 - 2.5 lbs ground chuck

½ a small onion, chopped

½ tbsp Lawry's seasoning salt

½ tbsp garlic powder

1 tsp cracked black pepper

1 pack King's Hawaiian rolls

4 slices of muenster cheese & yellow cheddar cheese

10-12 dill pickle chips

3 tbsp butter, melted

Sesame seeds for garnish

BIG MAC SAUCE:

⅓ cup mayo

2 tbsp ketchup

1 tbsp mustard

¼ tsp garlic powder, onion powder, smoked paprika

1 tbsp pickle juice

1 tsp Worcestershire sauce

DIRECTIONS

1. Season room temperature ground beef with Lawrys, garlic powder, cracked black pepper, and mix together (but don't over mix).

2. Add the ground beef to a 9x13 baking dish, evenly press it down to the bottom of the dish, and cook in the oven at 350°F for 20 minutes.

3. Mix together the ingredients to make the Big Mac sauce and put it in the refrigerator until it's time to use it.

4. Slice the Hawaiian rolls open and spray a new baking dish with cooking spray. Place the bottom buns in the baking dish and add on slices of muenster cheese.

5. When your meat patty is done, drain the oil and remove from the baking dish letting excess oil drip off the meat. Add the patty on top of the muenster cheese and blot meat dry with a paper towel.

6. On top of the meat patty add cheddar cheese slices, then chopped onion, and then dill pickles.

7. On the top buns evenly spread on the big mac sauce. Then top the sliders with the top buns.

8. Mix together melted butter, cracked black pepper, garlic powder, and sesame seeds. Brush butter mixture over the top buns. Cook in the oven at 350°F for 15-20 minutes.

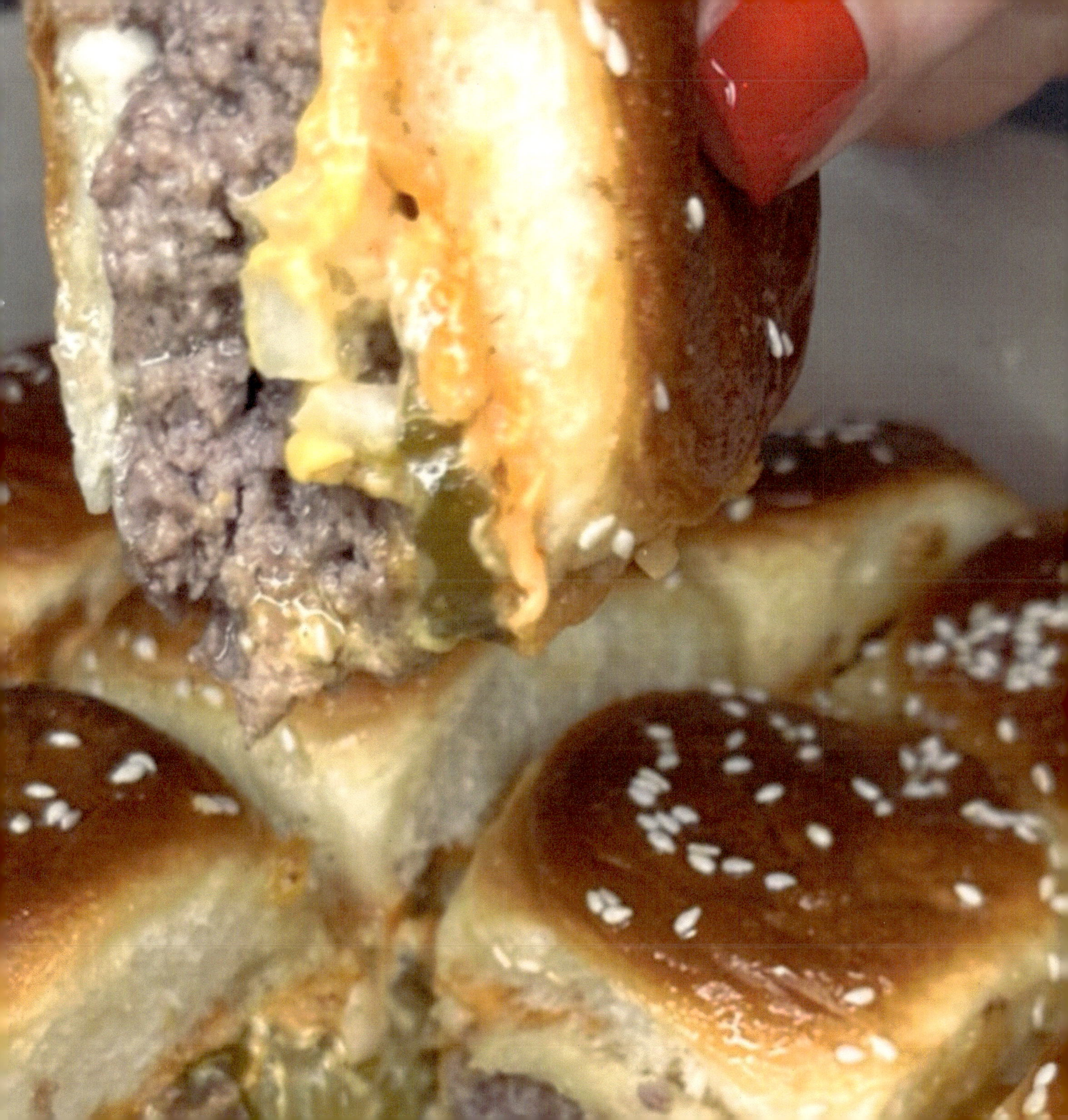

SAUSAGE & PEPPERS SLIDERS

SERVES 6-8

INGREDIENTS

1 lb hot ground Italian sausage

½ a red and green bell pepper, chopped

½ a small onion, chopped

3-4 cloves of garlic, chopped

1 pack King's Hawaiian rolls

1 tbsp olive oil

1 tbsp tomato paste

5 slices provolone cheese

2-3 oz freshly shredded mozzarella

10-15 sliced medium heat pepperoncinis

1 tsp kosher salt & cracked black pepper

½ tsp garlic powder

3 tbsp butter, melted

1 tbsp mayo

1 tbsp mustard

Pinch of cayenne pepper

DIRECTIONS

1. In a pan with olive oil add in ground sausage, chopped peppers, onion, garlic, salt & pepper, and sauté together on medium to high heat.

2. When the sausage is half way done add in tomato paste and brown for about 3 minutes.

3. Spray a 9x13 baking dish with cooking spray and slice open the Hawaiian Rolls, placing the bottom buns in the baking dish.

4. Start assembling the sliders by first adding to the bottom buns provolone slices, then the sausage mixture (when removing sausage from pan make sure to let the remaining oil drip out before placing it on the slider), then the pepperoncinis, then the freshly shredded mozzarella.

5. To make the sauce combine mayo, mustard, and cayenne pepper. Spread this sauce evenly over the top buns and then top the sliders with the top buns.

6. Mix together melted butter, garlic powder and cracked black pepper. Brush butter mixture over top of the sliders and cook in the oven at 375°F for 15 minutes covered and 15 minutes uncovered. Enjoy!!

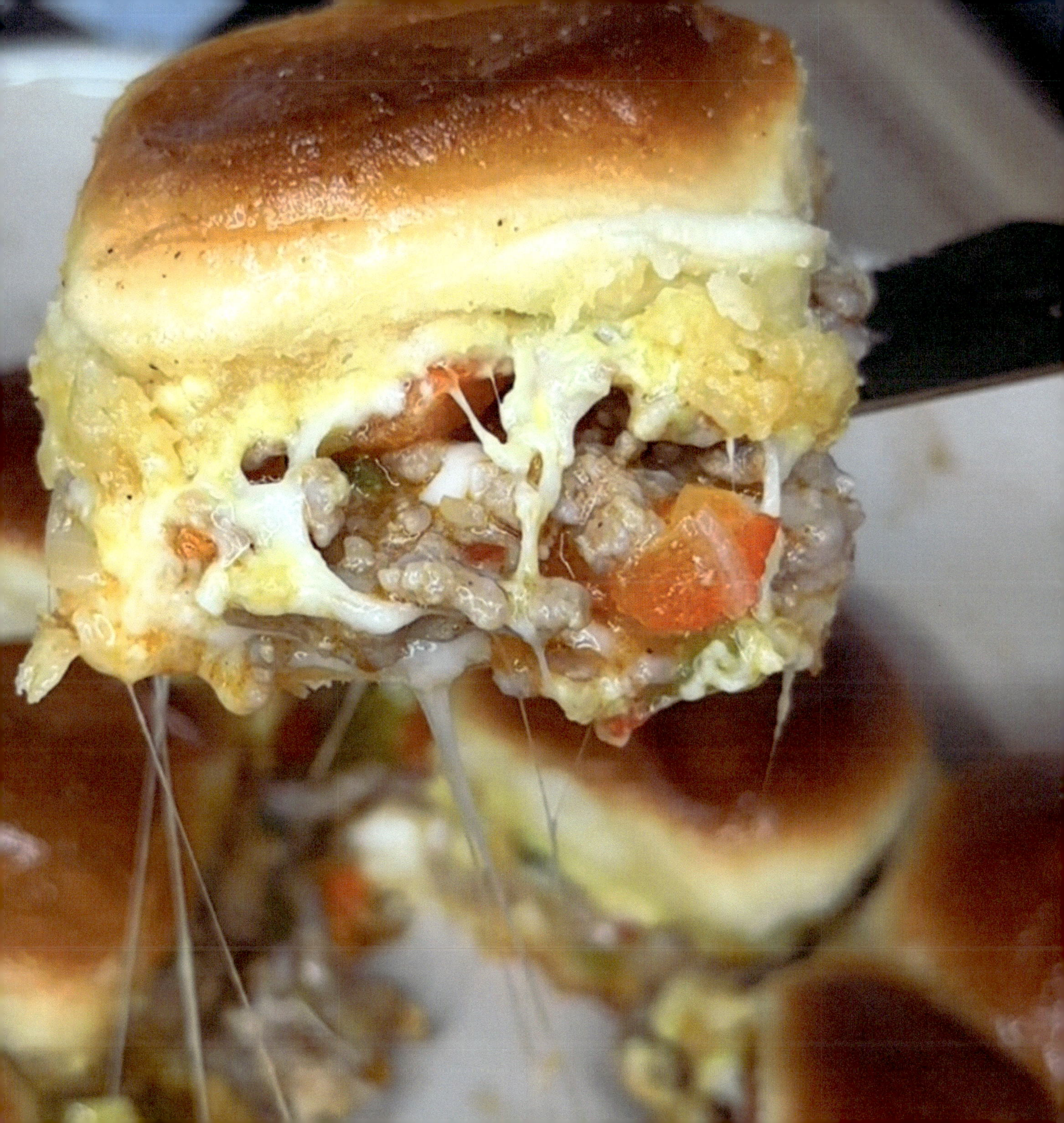

PIZZA SLIDERS

SERVES 6-8

INGREDIENTS

Sweet dinner sized rolls I use Hawaiian Rolls

¼ lb thinly sliced provolone

¼ cup of tomato basil marinara sauce

¼ lb thinly sliced deli sliced pepperoni

¼ cup of freshly shredded mozzarella

½ tsp of crushed red pepper

1 tsp of dried parsley

2 tbsp of grated Pecorino Romano + 1 tbsp. for the butter topping

½ stick of salted butter melted

2 tbsp of chopped fresh parsley and chopped fresh basil

2 cloves of chopped fresh garlic

About ½ tsp of each: salt pepper, garlic powder

Nonstick spray or butter for greasing the baking dish

DIRECTIONS

1. Slice open your rolls. Spray your baking dish with any nonstick cooking spray

2. Layer on bottom bun in this order: sliced provolone, tomato basil marinara, pepperoni slices, shredded mozzarella, crushed red pepper, dried fresh parsley, and 2 tbsp. of Pecorino Romano cheese.

3. Top the sliders

4. Prepare butter mixture by combining: melted butter, seasoning (salt, pepper, garlic powder), fresh chopped basil & parsley, chopped garlic, & 1 tbsp. of Pecorino Romano. Brush the butter mixture over the sliders

5. Bake at 350 for about 20-25 minutes total. Bake covered with foil for about 10-15 minutes. Then, uncover and bake for another 10 minutes until browned.

6. Remove from the oven and baste with a little more melted butter if needed.

7. Enjoy the best sliders ever!

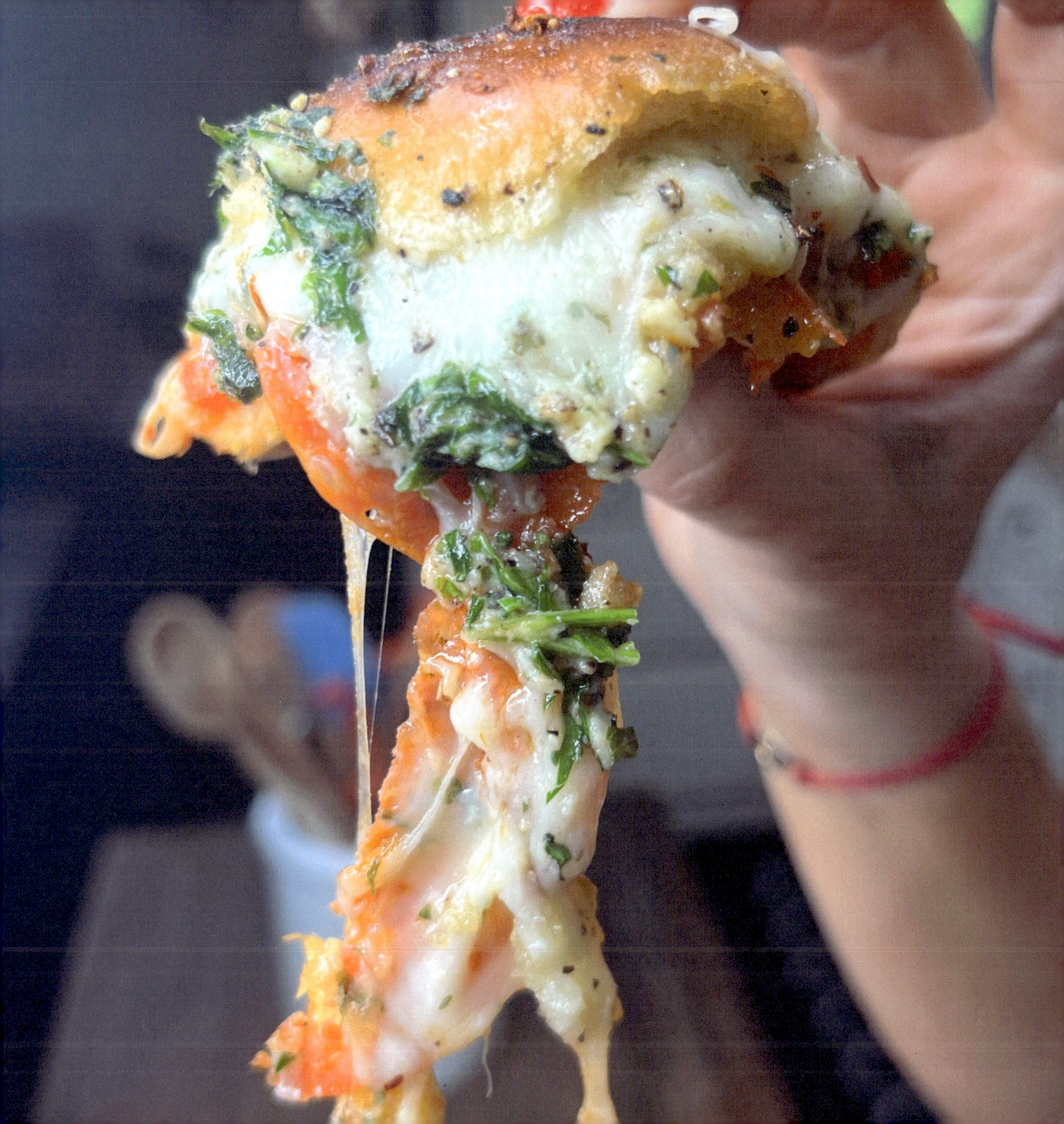

EASY CHEESY GARLIC BOMBS

SERVES 8-10

INGREDIENTS

1 can of Pillsbury Biscuit Grands, 8 count

About 2 sticks of salted butter, divided

2 tbsp honey

6-7 cloves of chopped garlic

About 2 cups of shredded cheese (I used Monterey jack, cheddar & mozzarella)

Seasoning: 1 tbsp of garlic powder, 1 tsp Italian seasoning, 1/4 tsp of chili flakes, salt and pepper to taste (always taste and add more if needed)

DIRECTIONS

1. With about 2-4 tbsp of butter grease a cast iron pan heavily, getting the bottom, sides, and corners.
2. Separate each biscuit lengthwise by pulling them apart to make two thinner biscuits. You should have 16 biscuits afterwards.
3. Melt about a stick and a half of butter in a measuring cup. Once melted add the above mentioned seasonings, the fresh chopped garlic, and honey into the melted butter. Whisk together until incorporated.
4. Brush each biscuit with the butter sauce. Then add shredded cheese on top of the biscuit: About 1-2 tbsp of cheese on each. Fold the biscuit together into a little ball. Then, roll with two hands to seal closed.
5. Add them into the cast iron, but make sure they are all positioned very close together in the center of the cast iron pan.
6. Top with the remaining butter sauce and add the leftover cheese on top. Sprinkle over some parsley (fresh or dried)
7. Bake at 350° F for 25 minutes. Serve and enjoy! Make it!!

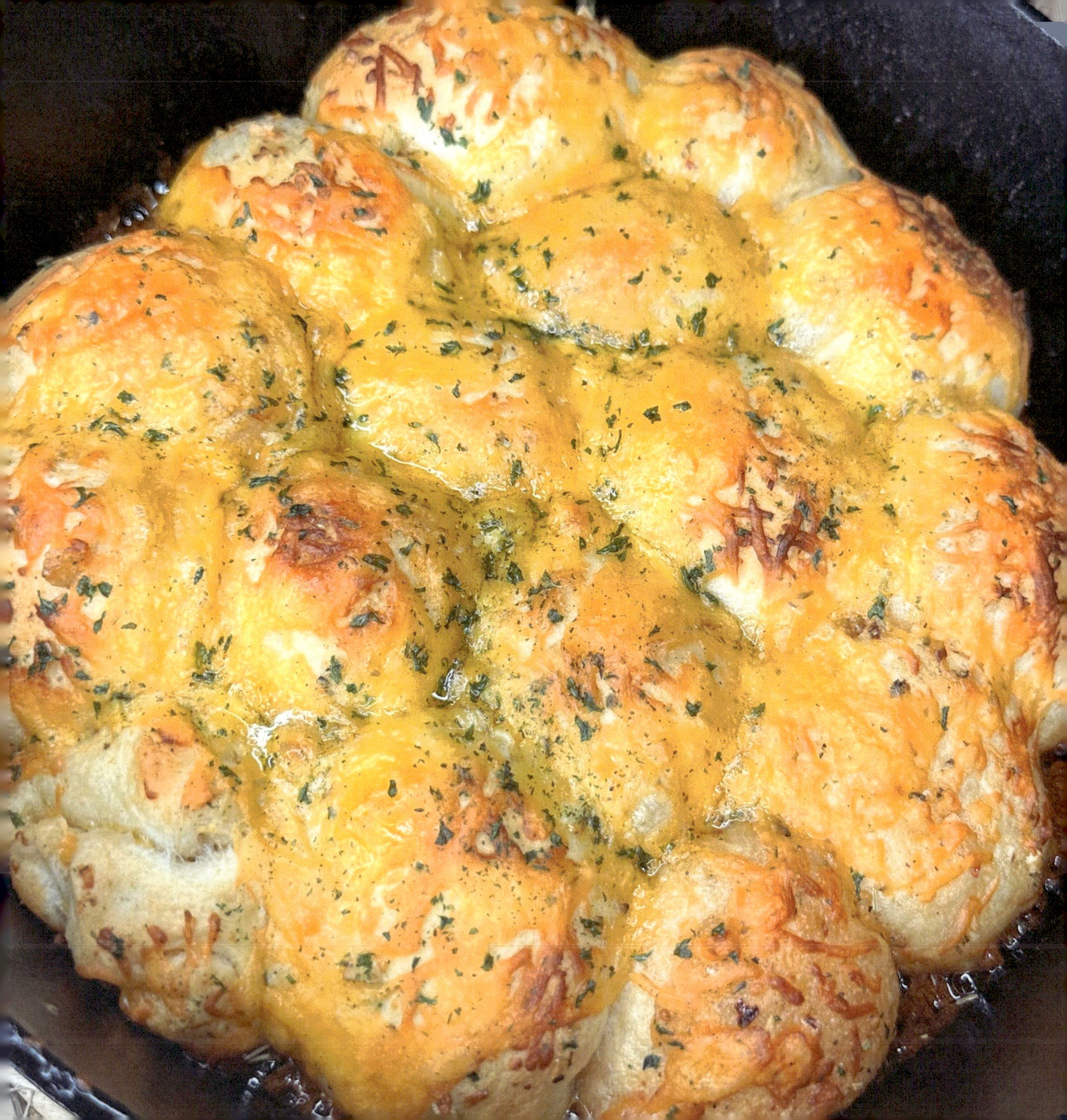

EASY ARTICHOKE DIP

SERVES 8-10

INGREDIENTS

3 (14 oz) cans of quartered artichoke hearts

11.5 oz of mayonnaise (1 squeeze bottle)

2 cups of freshly shredded mozzarella

½ cup of grated Pecorino Romano cheese

1 tsp of salt

2-3 tsp of cracked black pepper

1 tsp of crushed red pepper flakes

2-3 oz of freshly shredded gruyere cheese

DIRECTIONS

1. Grate the cheeses first and set them aside.
2. Add 3 cans of artichoke hearts into a colander and place the colander over a bowl. Squeeze all of the liquid out of the artichokes with your hands. Discard the liquid from the bowl as it fills with liquid. This will chop the artichokes to a perfect consistency as well.
3. Mix together the artichokes, mayonnaise, mozzarella, Pecorino Romano and seasonings. Add the dip to any size greased baking dish. Top with the shredded gruyere cheese and more cracked black pepper.
4. Bake in a preheated oven at 350° F for about 40 minutes or until lightly browned, melty, and bubbly. Enjoy!

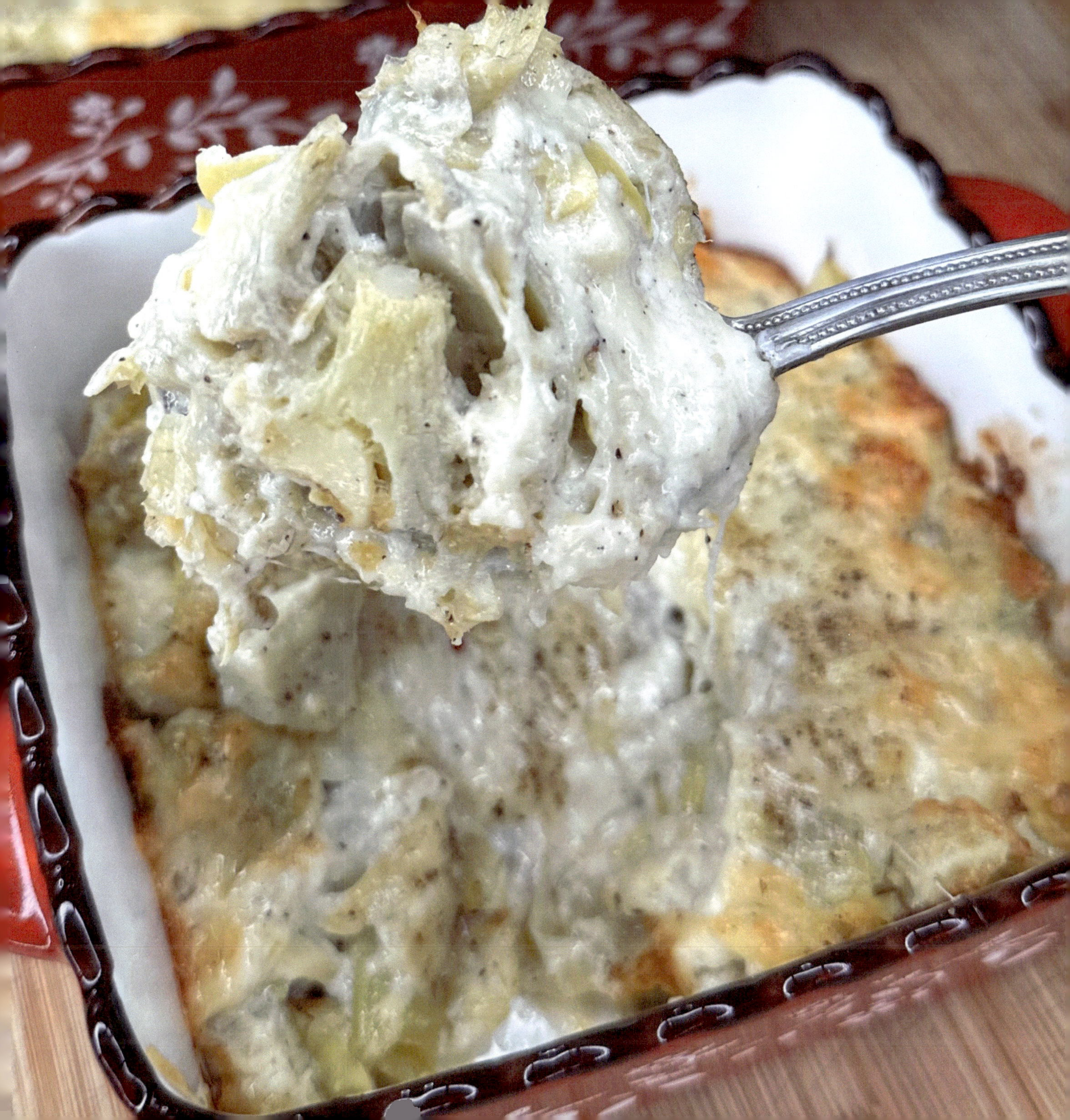

BIRDIE SANDWICHES

SERVES 6-8

INGREDIENTS

8 oz shredded cheddar cheese

4 oz can chopped black olives

½ a red onion, finely diced

4 tbsp of mayo

½ a stick of butter, melted

½ salt & pepper

1 tsp garlic powder

1 baguette

(Recipe from my dear friend Ninita)

DIRECTIONS

1. Mix together shredded cheddar (2 cups) cheese, 1 can of chopped black olives (4 oz), 1/2 Finely diced red onion, And about 4 tbsp of mayo (to bind ingredients together)
2. Toast English muffins or Italian bread and top with butter, salt, pepper, and garlic powder. VERY LIGHTLY toast in the oven at 350.
3. Remove from the oven and add the topping mixture.
4. Broil for 2-3 minutes until bubbly and melty! Serve and enjoy!

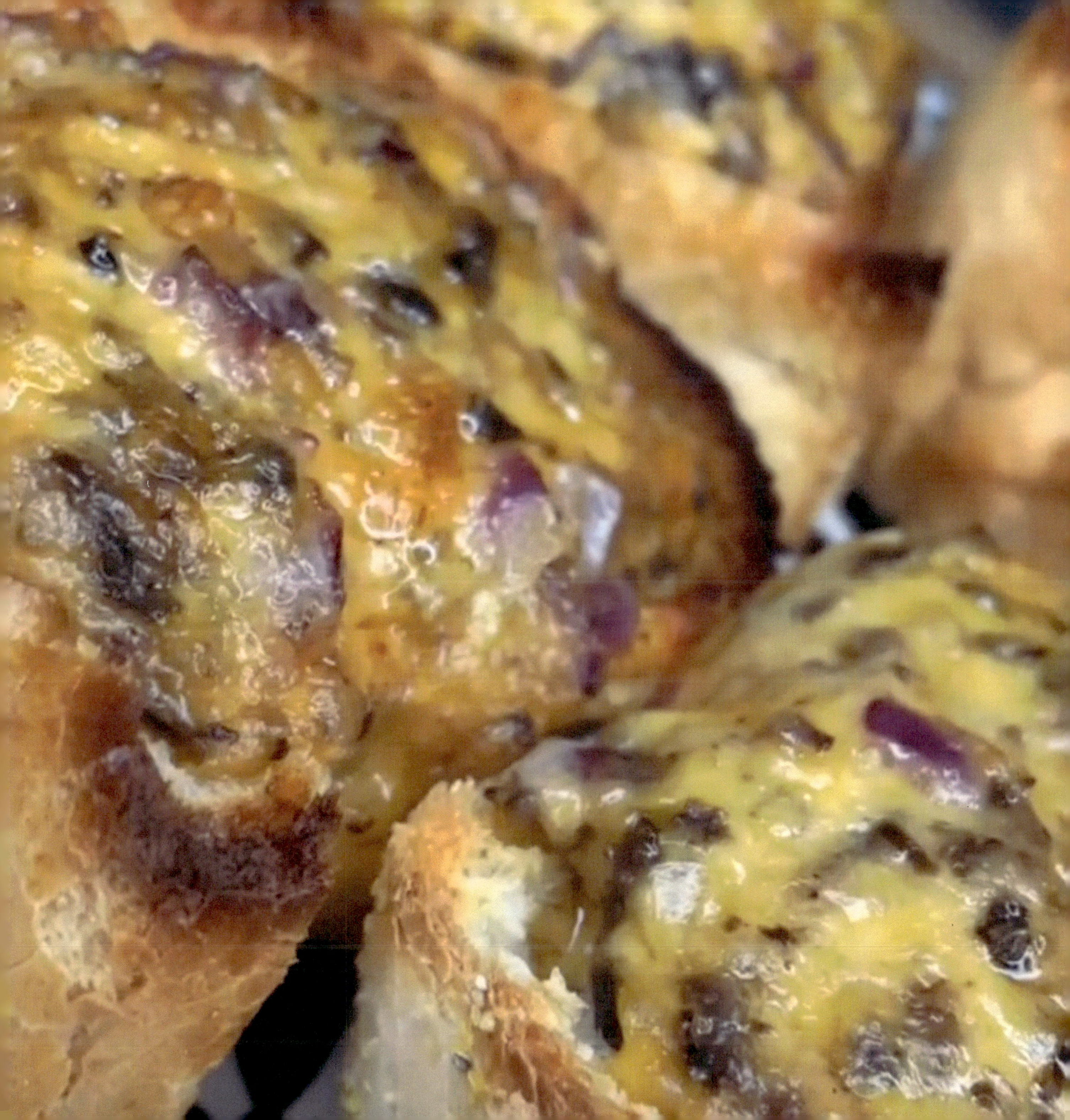

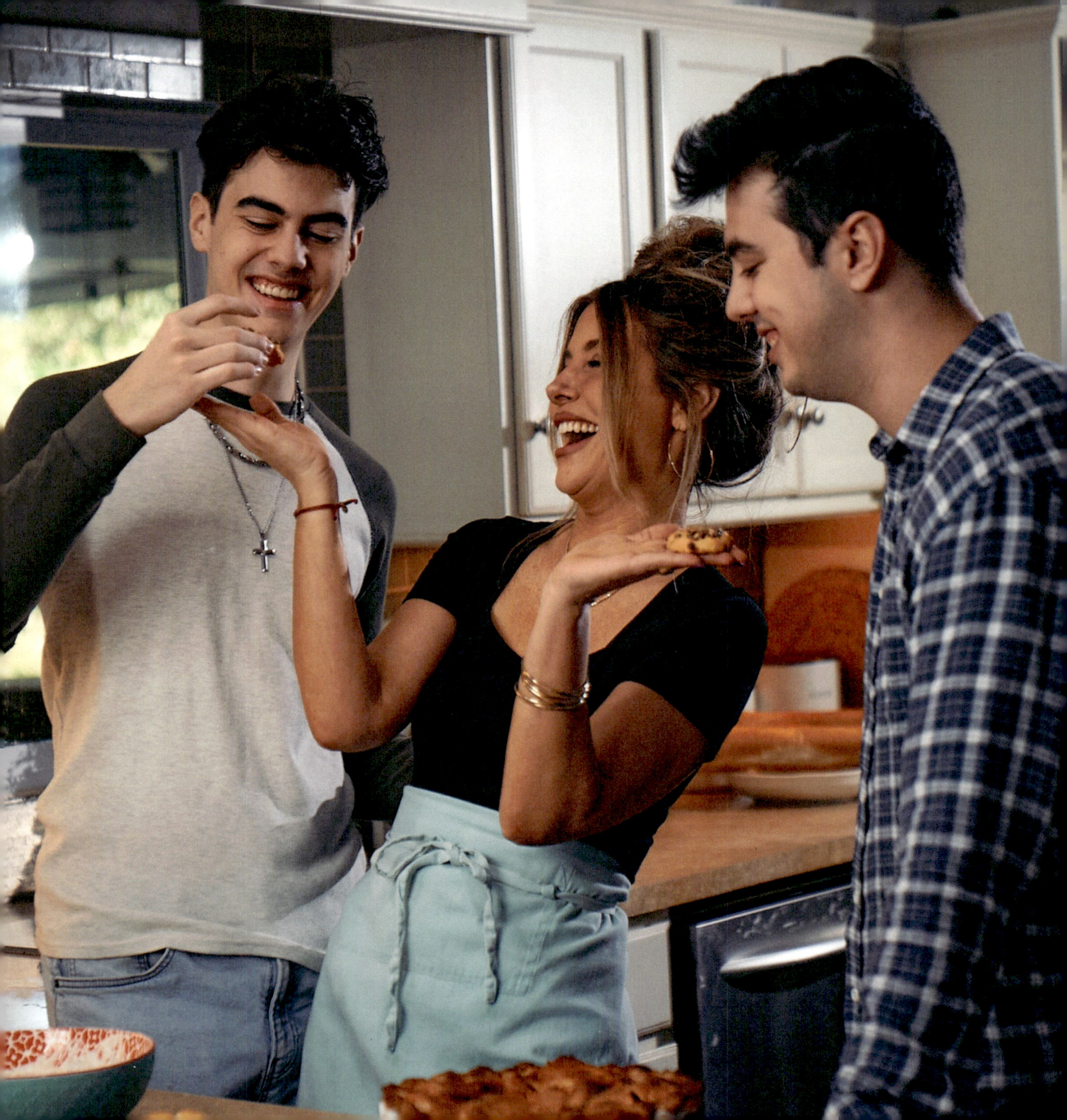

Desserts

CANNOLI POKE CAKE

SERVES 20

INGREDIENTS

1 box of french vanilla cake mix

1 cup of milk

2 sticks of butter, divided

3 eggs

1 tsp cinnamon

1 tsp cocoa powder

14 oz can of sweetened condensed milk

8 oz of mascarpone

½ cup of ricotta

1 tsp vanilla

½ cup of heavy cream

1 cup powdered sugar

Mini chocolate chips

Crushed waffle cones of cannoli shells

DIRECTIONS

1. In a bowl add cake mix (disregard box directions), 1 stick of butter melted, milk, cinnamon, eggs, and blend until combined.

2. Spray a 9 x13 with nonstick spray or grease with butter. Bake at 350°F for 28 minutes.

3. Mix together sweetened condensed milk with 1 tsp of cocoa powder and whisk.

4. As soon as you remove cake from oven poke holes 3/4 of the way through with the back of a wooden spoon. Pour the milk mixture over the top of the cake then sprinkle over a handful of mini chocolate chips.

5. Cover and refrigerate a couple hours before frosting.

6. To make the frosting blend mascarpone & 1 stick of softened butter for a few minutes, add ricotta & vanilla and blend another couple minutes, then add heavy cream and blend another couple minutes. Slowly add in powdered sugar and blend!

7. Frost the cake after a couple hours and top with more mini chocolate chips & crushed waffle cones or cannoli shells!

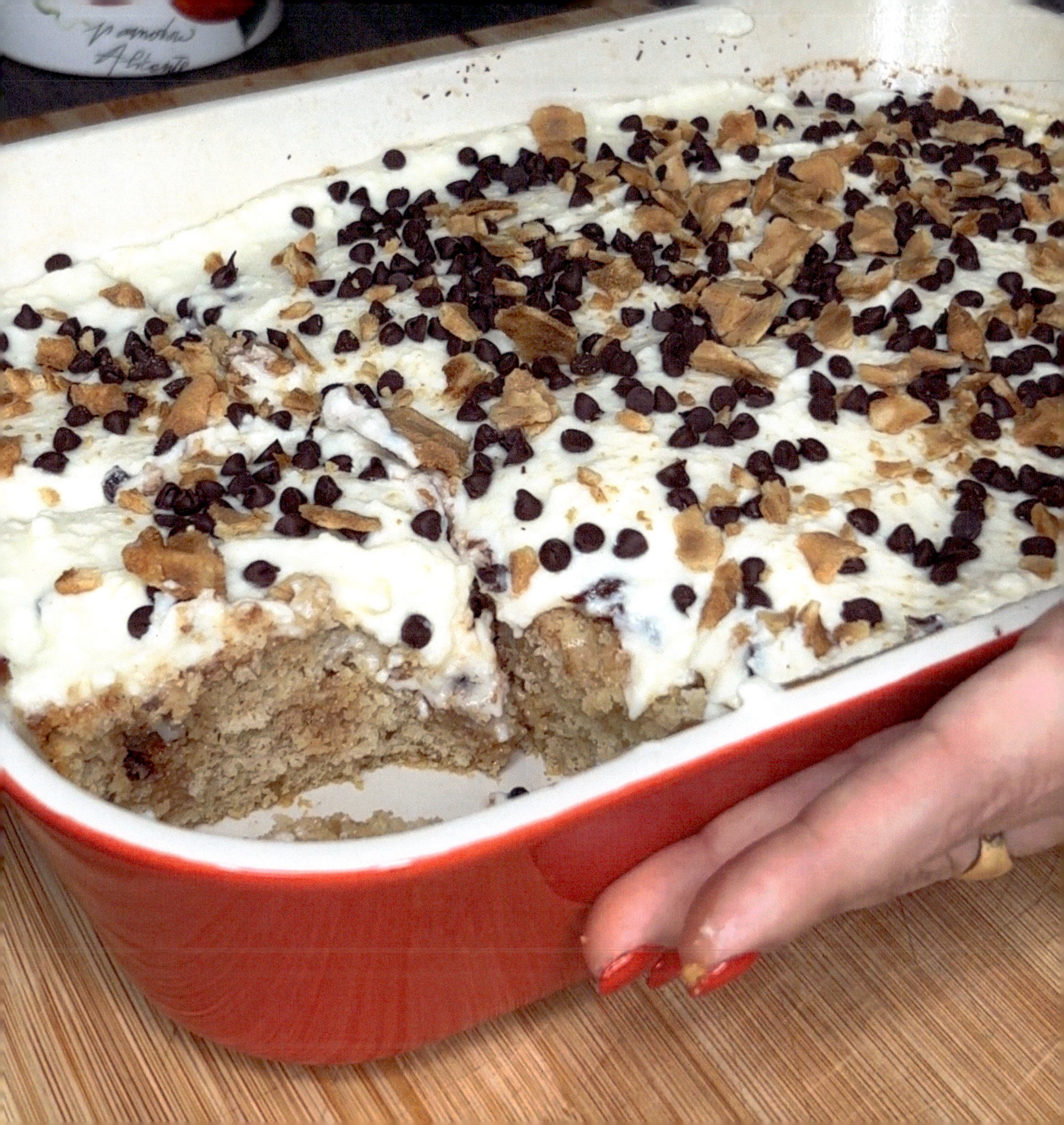

APPLE PIE

SERVES 8-10

INGREDIENTS

6-7 apples, peeled & sliced (2 red delicious, 3 Roma, 2 golden delicious)

14.1 oz pack Pillsbury pie crusts, both crusts

1 cup + 1 tsp sugar, divided

2 tbsp lemon juice

1 tsp cinnamon

½ stick of butter, diced

3 tbsp flour

¼ tsp ginger

½ tsp nutmeg

2 egg yolks

DIRECTIONS

1. Peel apples, slice them, and add them into a large bowl.
2. In the bowl add lemon juice, sugar, flour, cinnamon, nutmeg, ginger, butter, and mix everything together until incorporated.
3. Leave pie crusts out for 30 minutes to thaw out, then flour (about 3-4 tbsp of flour) your board and roll the dough out a little bit.
4. Add one dough to your pie dish and add your apple mixture in.
5. Then lay the second dough over top of the apples, pinch the dough together at the ends, and make a slit in the top.
6. Brush the entire top of the pie with the egg yolk and sprinkle sugar over the top (about 1 tsp).
7. Bake at 400°F for 1 hour, if the top starts browning early, put tinfoil loosely over the top halfway through cooking.

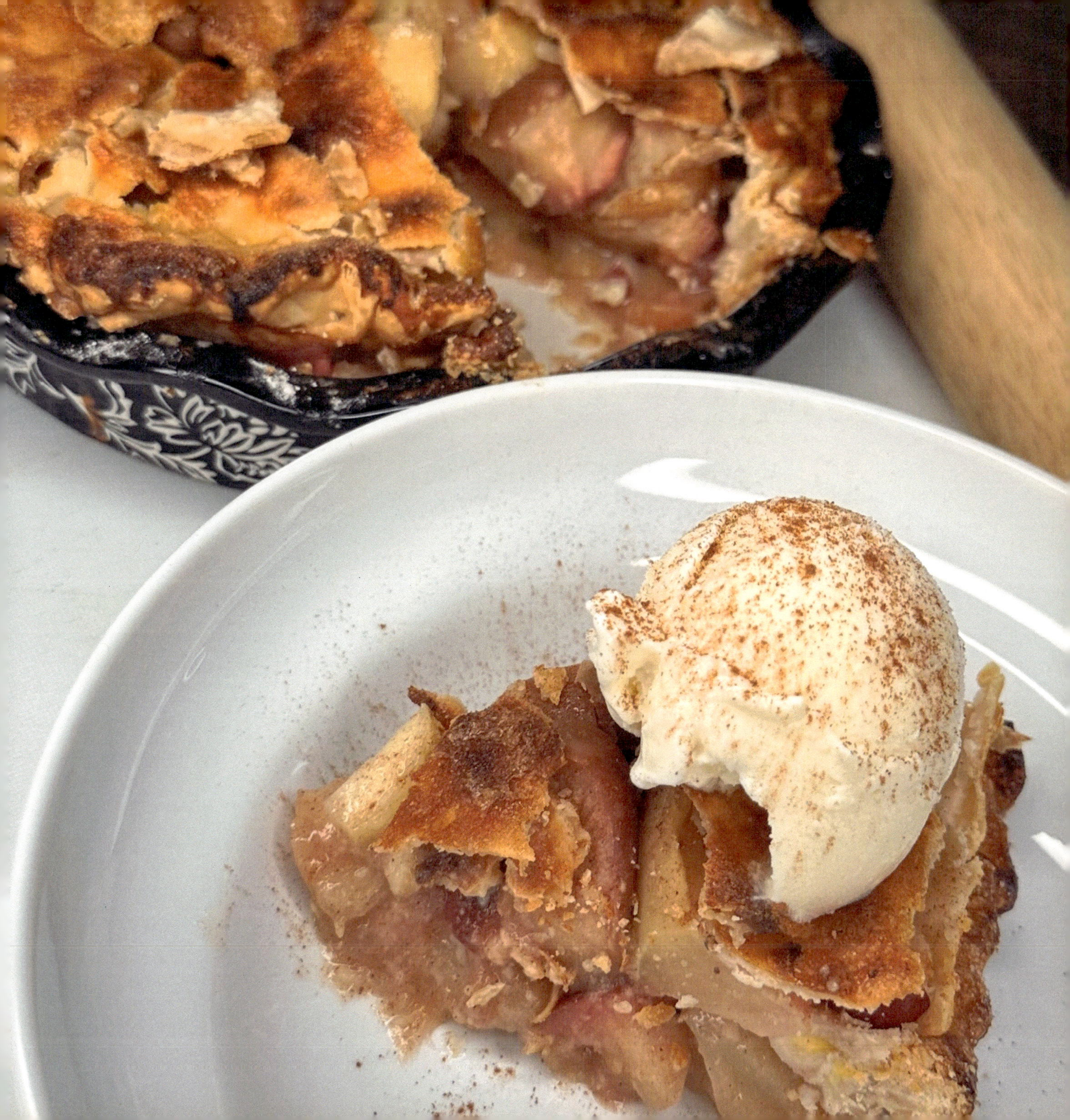

TIRAMISU POKE CAKE

SERVES 20

INGREDIENTS

1 box of vanilla cake mix disregard back of the box

1 cup of milk

3 eggs

1 stick of melted butter salted

1 can 14 oz of sweetened condensed milk

3 tbsp of brewed coffee

⅓ cup of Kahlua

1 tbsp of cocoa powder

1 tsp of espresso powder

WHIPPED ICING:

6-8 oz of mascarpone cheese

1 1/2 cups of heavy cream

½ cup of powdered sugar

3 tbsp of Kahlua

½ tsp espresso powder

DIRECTIONS

1. Preheat your oven to 350°F (175°C).
2. In a large mixing bowl, combine the vanilla cake mix, 1 cup of milk, 3 eggs, and the melted butter. Mix until well combined, ensuring no lumps remain.
3. Grease a 9×13-inch baking pan and pour the cake batter into it.
4. Bake the cake in the preheated oven for approximately 28 minutes or until a toothpick inserted into the center comes out clean.
5. While the cake is baking, prepare the coffee-Kahlua mixture. In a separate bowl, whisk together the sweetened condensed milk, brewed coffee, Kahlua, cocoa powder, and espresso powder until well combined. Set aside.
6. Once the cake is done, remove it from the oven and let it cool for a few minutes.
7. While the cake is still warm, use a fork to poke holes all over the surface. Make sure to only poke about ¾ of the way down, avoiding the bottom of the cake.
8. Slowly pour the coffee-Kahlua mixture over the cake, allowing it to seep into the holes. Continue pouring until the mixture is completely absorbed.
9. Place the cake in the refrigerator and chill for at least 1 hour to allow the flavors to meld together.
10. To prepare the mascarpone topping, beat the mascarpone cheese in a mixing bowl for approximately 3 minutes until smooth and creamy.
11. Add the heavy cream to the bowl and continue beating for about 5 minutes or until the mixture forms stiff peaks and resembles a frosting consistency.
12. Gently fold in 3 tbsp of Kahlua, ½ cup of powdered sugar, and ½ tsp of espresso powder until well combined.
13. Remove the cake from the refrigerator and spread the mascarpone topping evenly over the chilled cake.
14. For an elegant finishing touch, dust the cake with cocoa powder.
15. Slice and serve this luscious Tiramisu Poke Cake to savor the delectable flavors.

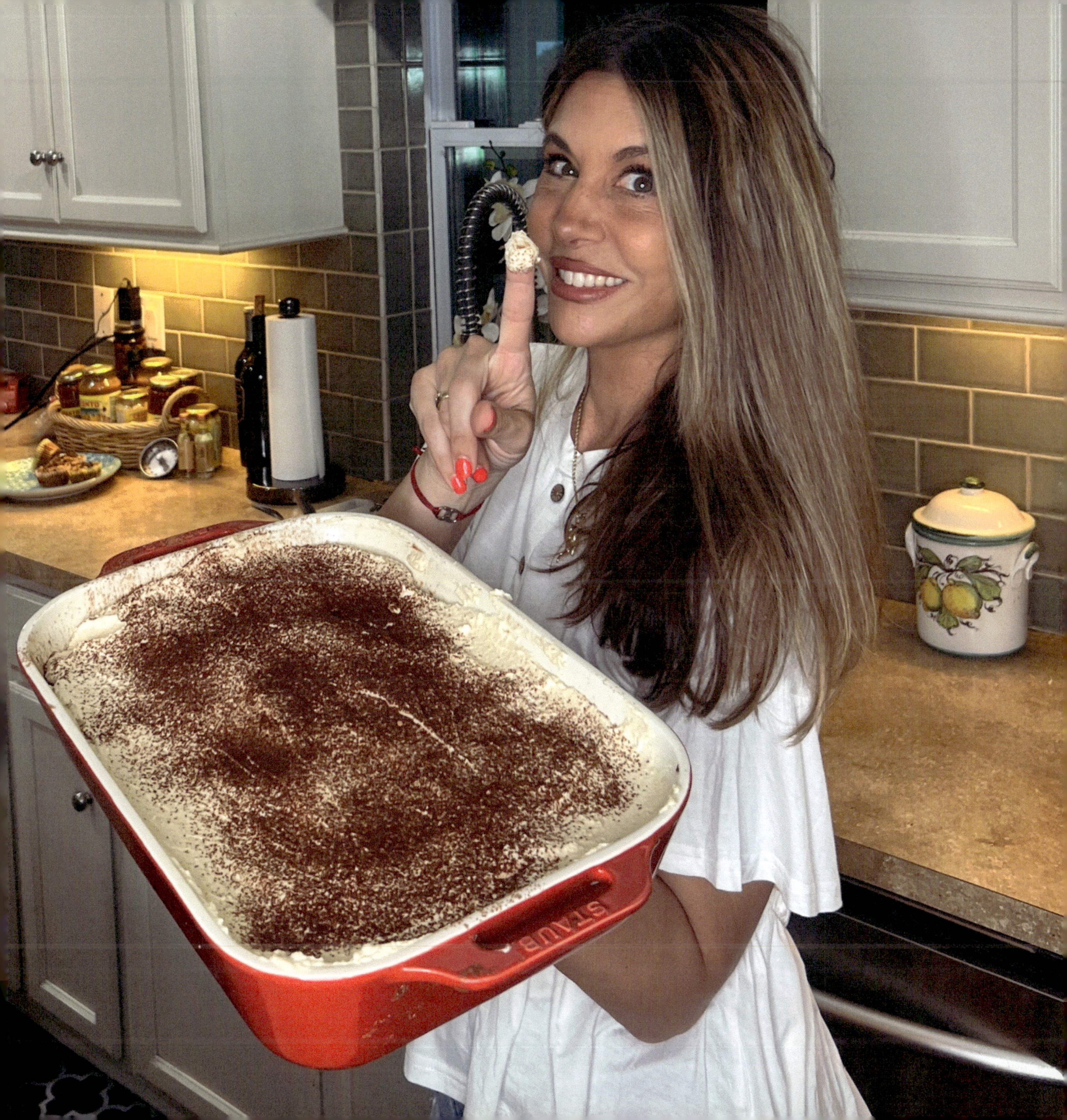
STAUB

HOT COCOA POKE CAKE

SERVES 20

INGREDIENTS

15.25 oz box of chocolate fudge cake mix

Ingredients on the back of the box including: 3 eggs, ½ cup of oil, and water

16 oz container of marshmallow fluff

¼ cup of water

2 cups of heavy cream

½ tsp of espresso powder

2 packets of hot chocolate packets (.73 oz. in each packet)

1 tsp of vanilla extract

Hot fudge

Maraschino cherries

DIRECTIONS

1. Bake the cake according to the instructions, but substitute 1 & 1/4 cup of water with 1 cup of water + 1/2 cup of Kahlua Liqueur.

2. Bake the cake at 350°F for 30-35 minutes in a 9×13 size baking dish.

3. Prepare the marshmallow by adding 1 container (16 oz.) of fluff in a microwave safe bowl and add 1/4 cup of water. Microwave for 20 second intervals and mix in between each interval. Keep doing this until you get a looser consistency.

4. As soon as the cake comes out of the oven while it is warm, poke holes in the cake using the handle of a wooden spoon. Poke the holes 3/4 of the way through the cake.

5. Pour the marshmallow mixture all over the cake.

6. Let the cake cool in the refrigerator for about 1 hour before adding the whipped topping.

7. Whipped topping: In a bowl add heavy cream, espresso powder, vanilla, and 2 packets of hot chocolate mix. Blend with an electric mixer until stiff peaks are formed.

8. Smooth the whipped topping over the cake.

9. Heat up hot fudge and swirl using a fork all over the cake & Add maraschino cherries as a garnish.

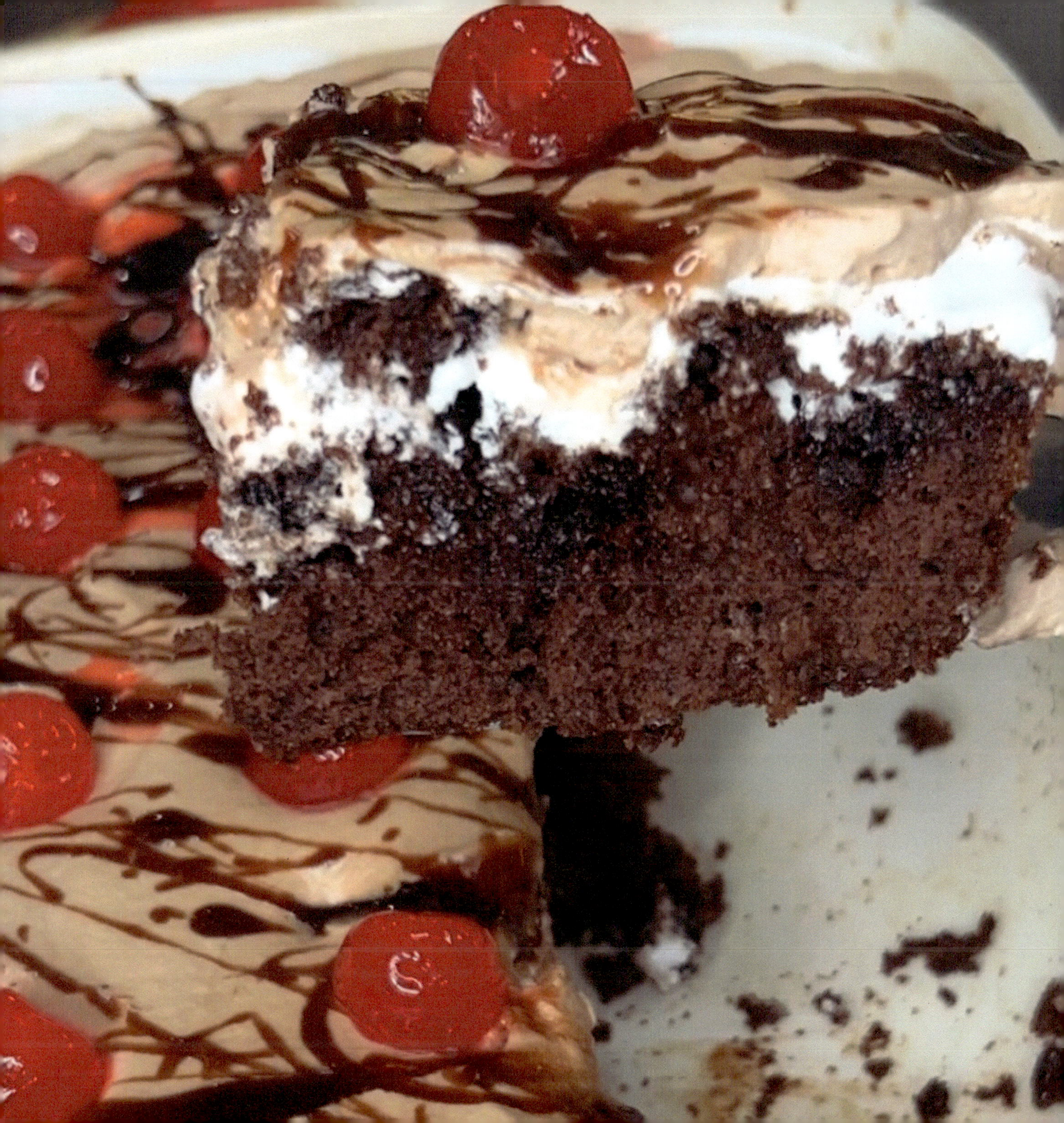

KEY LIME PIE

SERVES 8-10

INGREDIENTS

1 1/4 cups crushed graham crackers

½ cup sugar

⅓ cup melted butter

2 cans sweetened condensed milk

½ cup key lime juice I recommend Nellie and Joe's brand

Zest of ½ lemon

Juice of 1 lemon

3 egg yolks

DIRECTIONS

1. Begin by preparing the crust. You have two options: either crush graham crackers yourself or use pre-crushed graham cracker crumbs available in stores. Whichever you choose, you'll need 1 & 1/4 cups of crushed graham crackers.

2. In a mixing bowl, combine the crushed graham crackers, sugar, and melted butter. Mix well until the mixture holds together.

3. Press the crust mixture into a pie plate, ensuring an even layer at the bottom and up the sides. Pop it into the refrigerator and let it chill for about an hour.

4. To prepare the filling, In another bowl, combine sweetened condensed milk, key lime juice, lemon zest, lemon juice, and 3 egg yolks. Mix until combined.

5. Once the crust has chilled for an hour, pour the prepared filling into the pie crust, spreading it evenly.

6. Bake the pie in a preheated oven at 350°F (175°C) for about 30 minutes, or until the filling is set and slightly golden on top.

7. After baking, let the pie cool for an hour at room temperature. Then, transfer it to the refrigerator and let it chill for an additional 2 hours.

8. Once the pie has chilled, it's time to get creative! You can decorate it with a dollop of whipped cream, lime zest, or even a sprinkle of graham cracker crumbs. Let your imagination run wild! Slice & serve!!

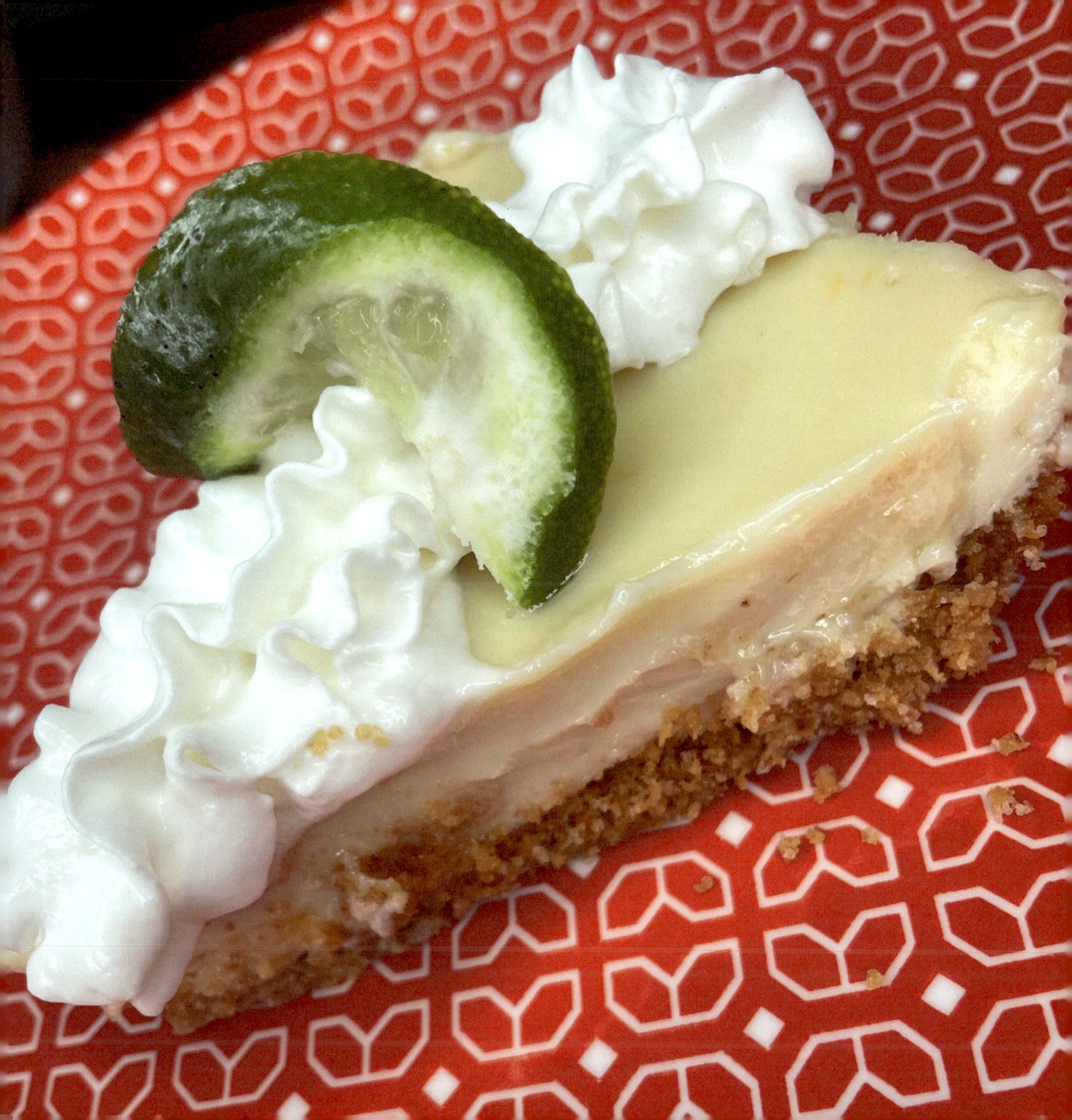

PINEAPPLE UPSIDE DOWN BUNDT CAKE

SERVES 12-15

INGREDIENTS

1 box of yellow cake mix

The 3 eggs & ½ cup of oil called for on the back of the box

Pineapple juice from canned slices instead of the 1 cup of water called for on the back of the box we will replace that with the pineapple juice from the can. I only had enough with the 15.25 oz. can I bought to fill half a cup of pineapple juice, so I filled the other half with water. AND IT WAS AMAZING! But, buy the 20 oz. can so you can have all pineapple juice.

1 stick of salted butter, melted

½ cup of brown sugar

20 oz can of pineapple slices packed in 100% juice

6-7 maraschino cherries

Pam or butter to grease the bundt pan (use A LOT)

DIRECTIONS

1. Preheat your oven to 350°F (180°C).
2. In a mixing bowl, prepare the cake mix according to package directions, substituting the reserved pineapple juice for an equal amount of water.
3. In a separate bowl, mix the melted butter and brown sugar together.
4. Pour the butter and brown sugar mixture evenly into the bottom of a greased bundt pan.
5. Arrange the pineapple slices in a single layer over the butter and brown sugar mixture.
6. Place one cherry half in the center of each pineapple slice.
7. Pour the cake batter evenly over the pineapple slices.
8. Bake for 40-45 minutes, or until a toothpick inserted into the center of the cake comes out clean.
9. Remove the cake from the oven and let it cool for 5 minutes.
10. Invert the bundt pan onto a serving platter and let the cake cool completely.
11. Serve and enjoy!

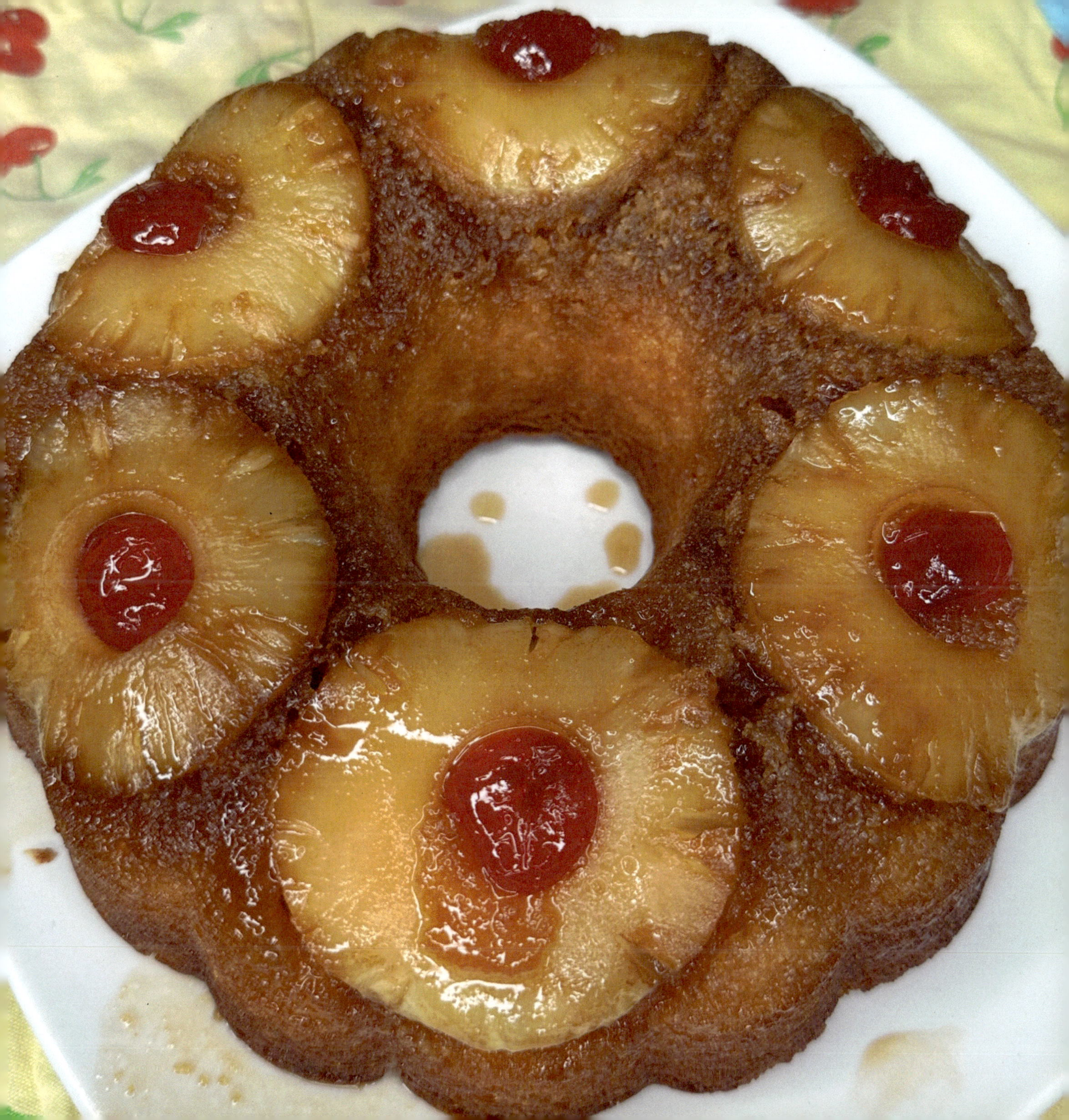

ACKNOWLEDGEMENTS

I would be remiss if I did not acknowledge the key players who helped me get here today. I started this journey with my sons' Nicholas and Anthony during the pandemic just to have a little fun on social media.

My sons, Anthony and Nicholas recorded my every move for the first two and a half years of this entire experience; every single day without fail. Both sons jumped in front of the camera with charisma to happily support me!

A heartfelt thank you to my Mother and late Grandma Jo who shaped me into the woman I am today, by giving me loving advice and confidence which stems from the hard working Italian women from generations past. Special acknowledgement to my sister, aunts, family, and friends for all their support as well.

Very importantly to all my fans and supporters that made my dreams come true with all their likes, comments, shares, and especially when they make it!!! With this book I hope I can bring joy and happiness to your kitchen and all your family meals.

A special thank you to precious Riley Roux Sous, my assistant, and surrogate daughter. Also to BJ Golnick for the professional pictures used of me throughout this book, I truly appreciate you...

Now... You know what you have to do... Make it!!!!